INSIDE OUT

BUILDING A GLASS HOUSE IN RUSSIA

INSIDE OUT

GLENN WILLIAMSON

Archway Publishing books may be ordered through booksellers or by contacting:

Archway Publishing
1663 Liberty Drive
Bloomington, IN 47403
www.archwaypublishing.com
1-(888)-242-5904

Because of the dynamic nature of the Internet, any web addresses or links contained in this book may have changed since publication and may no longer be valid. The views expressed in this work are solely those of the author and do not necessarily reflect the views of the publisher, and the publisher hereby disclaims any responsibility for them.

Certain stock imagery © Thinkstock.
Any people depicted in stock imagery provided by Thinkstock are models, and such images are being used for illustrative purposes only.

ISBN: 978-1-4808-0525-5 (e)
ISBN: 978-1-4808-0524-8 (sc)

Library of Congress Control Number: 2014901475

Printed in the United States of America

Archway Publishing rev. date: 2/12/2014

For Lyuba, and all those who inspired me to keep going.

CONTENTS

PROLOGUE:
THE GRANDFATHER

"I... understand the weakness of our position," he said in Russian. (*Ya ponimayu slabosti nashi pozitsiy.*)

Sweating through his collar, his heavy face bright red, Grigory Kleptov spoke slowly and meekly across the small, round black wooden table to begin our meeting with the two contractors. They were impatient. We were meeting after hours in the cramped office our joint venture had established in an old apartment while we oversaw the development of a modern office and retail center across the street on Krasotsky Prospect. Kleptov, my Russian codirector, was theoretically on my side, protecting my flank. Two against two. Owner versus contractor. *Thanks a lot, kemo sabe*, I thought.

We were in the middle of a basic dispute with these contractors over a drawing. Did it show a *water-resistant* or a *waterproof* basement floor? There was a lot of money at stake, probably several hundred thousand dollars out of a subcontract worth a few million. The Russian contractor had priced his proposal with the idea that the floor would be water-resistant, but we wanted waterproof. Most likely, he had assumed water-resistant and hadn't noticed that the official drawing said waterproof in English. He may not have understood the difference.

In St. Petersburg, any given year experiences thirty freeze and thaw cycles. When the frozen swampy ground begins to thaw each spring, tremendous pressure pushes up on the bottoms of the foundations of historic buildings, resulting in a big risk of flooding. Later on with this particular job, we would specify and pay for what would be labeled as runway concrete—an extra-thick concrete floor bolted to the brick foundation walls with steel angles to hold it in place. For now, though, we were finishing the demolition work and just wanted to secure the building for the future construction. A water-resistant basement would be half-assed and surely result in more cost and hassle in the future.

Kleptov had negotiated this particular contract over the summer, before I arrived in September 1995. Harry Marin, our seasoned American construction director at Walton Development, had been furious when he found out about it. Harry acted furious over everything as a normal state of affairs, like today being Tuesday or my being younger than him. But he was especially furious about this particular contract.

"He's on the take," Harry screamed at me in one of our first meetings, "and there's nothing we can do about it!"

The contractors were furious that they had to meet and discuss this issue, and were indignant at Kleptov for not holding up his side of the bargain. Why should they have to waste their time meeting with a young American assistant director when they had already taken care of the senior Russian general director? And worse, we weren't going to talk about money or favors. I was just interested in doing my job on behalf of the joint venture. Our job. The basement floor should be built as it said in the contract, and the drawing was part of the contract. That's what we were paying for. I was young, only thirty-three, and inexperienced with nuances of construction, but the issue seemed pretty basic.

The lighting was terrible in that shitty old apartment. The main contractor had a dark and frankly evil look, even if he were standing on a sunny street in May—and in this dusky setting late in November, the look on his face was that much worse.

Harry Marin had demanded this particular meeting, but he was managing the construction project while flying back and forth from St. Petersburg to his home near San Francisco. Kleptov and the Russian contractors simply waited him out during his visits and then took action whenever he left town. When Harry returned, they played dumb. Harry was extremely knowledgeable and effective in the field of construction, with decades of experience on major Walton developments across the United States and in Poland. For some reason, he always acted as if he hated me. The Golden Boy, he later called me with a sneer after we had successfully renegotiated some agreements. I grew to hate him as well over the course of the project, because he never seemed to understand we were on the same team. Still, I will always be indebted to him for convincing me to go home to make sure I was present for the birth of my oldest son. Ironically, Harry pushed me because he had missed the birth of his own daughter years earlier so he could attend the big pour of concrete on a project he was responsible for.

So the upshot was, Harry wasn't in St. Petersburg that day, and we needed to make a decision.

Walton's construction site manager, Richard Bruce, would normally handle these types of contractor disputes, but Richard was in prison. He had been arrested for tax evasion. He was a strong, tough-talking Australian with a black belt in karate. He didn't take grief on the site. But maybe he was a little overconfident. When I had been a foreign-service student, I was taught to be more cautious and less cocky. I first studied Russian in what was then Leningrad in the 1980s. My Georgetown professors told me and my fellow students that we should never, ever sign any *protokol* if we were ever taken to a police station. We were to say that we didn't speak Russian and ask for help. Never sign anything. Richard missed that lesson. Prior to serving as our site manager, he worked as his own contractor renovating apartments to lease to expatriates, or expats. When he signed the *protokol* at the police station, denying everything they were accusing him of, he created a document that conflicted with some invoices the police already had, so it meant they could hold him in jail. He spent three months in the infamous Krestyani prison until he was finally able to sort it out.

Richard's bad luck had started less than two weeks after he had slurred "Ayehm more Russian than you ahrr!" in his thick Australian brogue to one of our senior Russian partners, Alexander Slova. I had never been or seen anyone else as drunk as we all were that night. Kleptov had just become a grandfather, and a small group of coworkers were finishing the last of five bottles of Metaxa, a Greek brandy that tasted to me like a hacksaw blade. We laughed at Richard's boast. It was priceless.

But then, through the fog of our laughter, I heard him go on and realized he was serious. "My family were Cossacks," he said. "We were driven out by Communist scum like you seventy years ago."

Oh my God, I thought. *He's the site manager and he's talking to a board member from our major partner.*

Russia is a superstitious place, and if nothing else, it wasn't a good move for him to burn bridges with potential allies.

"You have my condolences," the company attorney for Neptune, our Russian business partner, told me later when I asked for his help getting Richard out of jail.

So with Harry out of the country and Richard in jail, I had to handle today's meeting. I could speak Russian. Not perfectly, but certainly well enough, I thought, to manage this simple conversation. Neither Kleptov nor the contractors would have accepted having a translator there anyway. We had an excellent translator on staff, but Kleptov would not have wanted her there to watch him sweat. Awkward. Not very becoming for the general director. So Kleptov and the contractors flattered me and said we'd meet, just the four of us, and hold the meeting in Russian since my language ability was so good.

I was the assistant director of Krasotsky 23, our joint venture company. My US employer, Walton Development, owned 9 percent of the joint venture and served as the developer. As developer, we were responsible for managing the construction process on behalf of the joint venture and especially on behalf of Urobank, the main Western shareholder. The other major shareholder was a serious Russian investor, Neptune Design, a Russian naval design firm that had built the Red October submarines. Neptune had nominated Kleptov to be general director of the joint venture based on his earlier position in the St. Petersburg city administration, but the leaders at Neptune never seemed to appreciate all of the extracurricular activities Kleptov was involved in. Not until later.

So on this day I was responsible but not empowered. I knew my counterpart, Kleptov, was actively working at cross purposes—in my view—to getting our project built to the Class A standards we had promised to deliver. I was beginning to see how his various side deals created enormous distractions to our main purpose. And I could never figure out who the people endlessly parading in and out of his small private room in our office were.

From Kleptov's point of view, I just didn't understand how things worked or what really mattered. I'll never forget how he once came back to the office flushed with pride, tipsy from lunch, and just as red and sweaty as today but in a much more jovial mood. He showed me a single piece of paper, a form of some kind inside a clear plastic sleeve. It had thirteen separate stamps on it. I don't think I could even make out what the form was behind all the red and blue stamps.

Kleptov waved it around and thrust out his barrel chest. "I did it." He beamed. "Finally, I have it! They have approved the design of the gas pipe."

INTRODUCTION

"Real estate or Russia?" the would-be publisher asked me. "What is your story about? Where does it fit in?" When my firstborn son was two weeks old in 1997, I started to write a book for him called *A Gift for Charlie*. I wanted to tell him what I had learned in my life. At that time I thought I had already learned a lot. I was well educated. My work was interesting. I was trying to make a difference.

After finishing Georgetown's School of Foreign Service in 1983, I had applied to the US Foreign Service. With Reagan in office, the Cold War was heating up and I spoke Russian. I aced the written exam but failed the personality test, twice. So I volunteered to teach in Tijuana, Mexico, and learned Spanish. Then I got an MBA at the University of Chicago and began my career, redeveloping properties in Chicago's neighborhoods. Chicago's commercial real-estate markets collapsed in the early 1990s, just after the Berlin Wall fell. It was a good time for me to remember that I spoke Russian. That part of the world was changing fast. Chicago developers were taking notice. My wife was up for the challenge.

From 1995 to 1998, I lived in St. Petersburg, managing the redevelopment of a historic landmark—former monks' apartments—into one of that city's premier office and retail centers, The Atrium at Krasotsky 23. This joint venture was led by a Chicago developer on behalf of international partners from Russia, the United Kingdom, and the United States. We turned the old buildings inside out. The process turned all of us inside out as well. Hence the book title.

I wound up living overseas for ten years in Central and Eastern Europe (CEE). Returning home to the United States in 2003, I formed my own company, Amber Real Estate, and continued to fly back to CEE, mostly to Poland. Amber closed a number of deals as these emerging markets became less exotic and investors became more comfortable with the projects. I began to teach a course at Georgetown, based on what I had learned and the stories I had been part of. By far the best stories came from Russia.

My book, though, sat for fifteen years. Last year, I picked it up again to fill in some spare time and to finish the tale before I forgot all the details. My family was living in Washington, DC. My older son Charlie was a sophomore at a wonderful and challenging school in DC. His younger brother, David, was eight and enrolled at the same small school. My wife and I were going through our divorce. When the boys were away with her on our alternating weekends, I used the time to finish my story of the Atrium. No pure good guys or bad guys, just a lot of interesting, committed, and imperfect people. Maybe a little more reality than a morality play.

I wrote the book to share what I think I learned about real estate and Russia. Promise and performance. I have changed the names, but the story is realistic—as best as I can tell, as I saw it, working in the middle of it and looking out at all sides.

CHAPTER 1

THE PLANE BACK

I sank back in my seat as the plane took off from O'Hare Airport. As a new father, I had flown home to Chicago a few days earlier for the baptism of my son, in March 1997, and was now on my way back to Russia. Our joint venture in St. Petersburg had finished the demolition and preparatory work, and we hoped construction would finally move ahead with the final building—after we had worked out all the issues with the contractor, the financing, and the endless, endless permits.

Flights to Europe always left Chicago in the evening. That meant a lot of running around before getting to the airport at the end of the day. I had the compact video camera my parents, the new grandparents, had just given me. I would promptly lose this camera when switching planes in Frankfurt the following morning. Just lose it. Forget where I stored it because I was so tired. No baby videos to send home after all. But now, just after takeoff from O'Hare, I settled back, thinking everything was in its place. I had a glass of wine, pulled out a page from my priority manager, and started to write.

I only wrote one page. I labeled it *A Gift for Charlie*, thinking I'd fill it with advice I could give my newborn son when he got older. "You are only two weeks old as I write this, but your eyes are curious …"

⌒═══╪═══⌒

My flight back to Chicago for the baptism had not started well three days earlier in Russia.

Fat smiling guard, I thought when I was stopped at the customs security check, *with your stupid little pistol tucked under your belly. What are you going to do with that, shoot me?*

He told me I was going to miss the plane. "I am not missing the plane," I said right back in Russian.

If I missed this early morning flight, I would miss the only connection back to the United States that day and miss the baptism of our son, in which case my wife would surely kill me. The fat border guard was the least of my concerns.

"What is the problem?" I asked.

"You didn't declare this money on your form, so you can't take it with you."

Like an idiot, I had told Kleptov I would bring his son some dollars Kleptov had given me. His son was living in New York City. I kept that money separate from mine, tucking it in my shirt pocket. It wasn't an earth-shattering amount, but I hadn't declared it when sorting through the money in my wallet. Normally when passing through customs in Russia, you needed to declare each piece of currency you had. The theory was that the authorities could compare it with the foreign currency declaration you made when you entered the country, last week, last month. Didn't matter. If you had foreign currency, it must have come in with you. Forget cash stations, etc. Rules take a while longer than technology to change. And what the hell, the regulations this time worked. I was snared in the act!

"Come on," I told the guard, "what difference does it make?"

"No," he said.

A matter of principle on his part? Not likely.

He stared at me for a minute. Finally, he shook his head slowly in frustration and disbelief. I could practically read his thoughts. *What is it about these Americans? So thick sometimes.*

"Just leave one hundred rubles on the table," he said quietly.

About twenty bucks. Fine. I picked up the other bills and left a hundred rubles on the table. He smiled and waved me on. I bundled up my things—computer, carry-on, etc.—and hustled through the Soviet-era terminal that had only been partially upgraded at that point. Quasi tractors still pulled boarding buses to the plane every once in a while when they ran out of working buses.

This was becoming a tough morning. I had slept late and therefore was late getting to the airport. I was alone in the apartment in St. Petersburg, trying to push along the Atrium project after having been home for three weeks the previous month to be present for the birth of our son. That trip had worked out perfectly. I arrived home two weeks before Charlie was born and stayed one week after.

It was my fault I had slept late, but Georgi, my driver, hadn't been much help. He was sleeping out in the car waiting for me.

"Why didn't you call me?" I asked. "Or better yet, come upstairs?"

No answer. Georgi was dead lazy and would not have wanted to leave his warm car in that filthy dark courtyard so he could walk through the slush and up three flights of steps to ring the doorbell on my apartment.

I didn't even need a driver since I didn't have a car. I had inherited this guy with my position. Most of the time Georgi just read the newspaper. A month later, though, he showed true initiative, diligence, resourcefulness, and follow through.

After my wife and son's arrival in Russia, I realized that, yes, I would indeed need a driver as well as a car. My wife could then get rides to the stores, help with packages. Good. So I told Georgi to drive my wife around.

Not so fast, he said. It would be illegal for him to drive my car without me in it.

"Now you're a lawyer?" I asked him sarcastically.

So Georgi went to our company lawyer and had him draft a legal opinion that backed his position. I was astounded. Amazing initiative, albeit motivated solely by Georgi's desire to get out of work. And of course, Georgi was right. The temporary-import status of my Saab, which enabled me to avoid paying an import duty—and incidentally allowed me to present unintelligible Finnish documents to every Russian cop who pulled me over—restricted the use of the car to when I was physically present. Not my wife, just me.

To be fair, when I earlier announced to the staff that I needed to buy a car, Georgi offered to step up to the plate. "Glenn," he said, "I know how we can do this. Give me $10,000 and I'll go to Germany. I'll buy the car and drive it back for you."

"But, Georgi," I answered, "you don't speak German."

In the end I took a train to Helsinki with my wife and son and bought the ten-year old dark gray Saab 90 on my credit card for about $10,000. I had to call the Visa office to tell them not to worry and to approve the transaction, which they did. Normal, which was what I had always liked about Finland, dating to my first visits there on my way to and from Russia in 1981. Just normal. We drove the car back to Russia after spending the weekend in Finland. As long as I crossed back to Finland every six months or so—which we did anyway for getaway weekends—the car would be continually reexported and temporarily reimported to Russia.

When I first arrived in St. Petersburg in October, 1995, the Atrium project was in the midst of its demolition phase of the historic building. The building was actually four adjacent buildings built around a central outdoor courtyard. Originally constructed in the early 1800s, they had been living quarters for the monks serving at the neighboring Kazan Cathedral. By the 1990s, the building had fallen into disrepair like many of the historic edifices in St. Petersburg, but its location on Krasotsky Prospect made it a prime site for redevelopment. Although we were required to keep the original walls intact, we were demolishing the individual floors, digging a basement, and adding a new courtyard structure in order to support the planned redevelopment.

My assignment was to organize various subordinated loans from the joint venture partners, assist with securing and closing the primary loans from banks, and to gradually take over the project management in Russia. A development team typically consists of finance, construction, leasing, and property-management members. People and resources are devoted to each phase as the project moves from predevelopment, through design and construction, to leasing and operations. This is always a multiyear process, and the players on the team change as the project evolves or encounters particular difficulties. One person is always in charge of the team. That was me—project manager for Walton, the US developer, and simultaneously assistant director for the joint-venture Russian limited liability company, Krasotsky 23, which actually owned the project.

Two other Walton staff members were already on the ground in St. Petersburg—Richard Paul, the marketing and leasing manager; and Richard Bruce, the site manager who would soon be in jail. They were overseen by senior Walton directors based in Warsaw and supported by other senior US staff. Warsaw was the base of our Central Eastern Europe (CEE) operations because Walton had already completed a 100,000 square foot office building in 1993—the Polska Corporate Center—and was in the process of developing a high-rise Polska Financial Center comprising 700,000 square feet. The Polska Corporate Center had been a success because of timing, since it was built early in the demand cycle in Central Europe, when firms were hungry for space and there simply wasn't any to lease. The Corporate

Center was the first modern Class A office building completed in this market, and it was located next door to the Marriott Hotel, which served as the center of expat life. Its success had whet everyone's appetites for more projects. I understood from company legend that our building had been fully leased by eager international firms in about two weeks.

The leasing broker in St. Petersburg had been the property manager in Warsaw. He was eager for a similar success—and corresponding payoff—with the Russian project. He was older and less than fully receptive to the need for more local oversight of his activities. He was also frustrated. The modern glass Atrium building he was supposed to lease didn't have any glass or even a frame yet. It wasn't anywhere close enough to reality for him to discuss details, let alone sign leases. There was no delivery date in sight, and all he could do was hype a project with a moving occupancy date that was becoming a small joke in the tight-knit world of potential international tenants. He had seen leasing as a promotion from the day-to-day drudgery of property management, a chance to be a deal maker. "Leasing is the dream," Ralph Walton, our company founder, once reminded us, "but the reality is property management."

The lenders and partners at Urobank were also eager for quick success, in part to validate their stated mission to provide financing for Eastern Europe in general and Russia in particular. The annual meeting of Urobank's board of governors had been held in St. Petersburg a year earlier, in April, 1994, with few Russian projects to talk about. The Atrium project was conceived in that same time period. At the groundbreaking ceremony, the

mayor of St. Petersburg, Anatoly Sobchak, had toasted the goal
of completing the project by 1995.

My experience with Urobank prior to my joining Walton
had been enlightening. I was working in Bulgaria for South
Shore Bank, running a small-business loan program for their
affiliate, Shorebank Advisory Services. I knew South Shore
Bank from Chicago, where it was a leader in neighborhood
redevelopment on the city's South Side. The Bulgaria program was based on a similar and successful initiative run by
Shorebank in Poland. Urobank wanted Shorebank to expand
this same program across Russia, instantaneously. In 1995, I
was sent on an initial foray into Tula, a region south of Moscow
and famous as the location of Tolstoy's estate, Yasnaya Polyana.
I was feeling fairly important for a young banker. Urobank was
to send a car to meet me at the Moscow airport. Yes, that was
it, just what I deserved. The car turned out to be a gypsy taxi,
a typical beat-up car with a refrigerator-type magnet that said
taxi slapped on the roof when working. The driver took me from
Moscow to Tula, and as we pulled up to the hotel he asked me
for $240 in cash. I had just over $300 in my wallet. So much for
the red carpet. I paid him and wondered how I'd take care of
everything for the next two days. After all, I was there to help
launch the mighty Urobank-backed lending program. We had
meetings arranged with bankers and potential borrowers. And
I had $60. I suppose even if I still had the full $300, we weren't
going to change the world, but money was tight. There were no
cash stations in Tula then, and I had expected local expenses to
be handled by Urobank's local office, which didn't really exist.

After that trip I made sure to always keep a spare $100 bill tucked in my wallet.

So their one local representative and I hitched rides to meetings from random cars and tipped the drivers, a normal practice in Russia at the time. I was able to pay my two-day hotel bill using all of the money left in my wallet, since the hotel cost only $30 per night. That was a nice surprise, after I had waded through the hoary, frozen drunks in the casino that was part of the hotel lobby to check in. My wooden hotel door had a huge crowbar hole next to the lock that must have been on the to-do list for some years. And the hotel still employed *dezhurnayas*, the floor monitors that were the staple of Soviet hotels during Communist times. As a student in what was then Leningrad, I had experienced this system one summer in a cheap hotel. The *dezhurnayas* could bring you tea or your room key, and they also kept track of whoever came and went on each floor. Older, short, stocky, and tough as nails.

The day I arrived in Tula I watched our floor *dezhurnaya* shove two drunks down the stairs. Literally. They were trying to climb up from the casino to the floor with the rooms. No dice. Down they went. But they fit in well with the zany details that passed for normal in Russia at the time. Like masonry workers working outside in ten-degree weather with wet mortar, thoroughly mixed with industrial salts so it wouldn't freeze. ("Why do our buildings not last?" "Go figure!") Or the hand towel placed outside the bank, saturated in the half inch of fresh gritty sand loaded onto the sidewalk each morning so people wouldn't slip. Hundreds of people shuffled through the door, but someone had thought to put the hand towel there to manage the situation. Most people obliged by using it, surely stepping off the towel with more sand on their shoes than when they stepped onto it.

Back in Chicago, I shared my Tula stories with the younger recent college graduates whom Shorebank was recruiting and rotating over to Russia to run the loan programs. A distinct image formed in my head as I spoke to them, of a WWII paratrooper plane nearing its drop zones. As each young banker was shoved out of the plane, the officer would look at his map and announce over the radio to Urobank HQ in London that yet another loan office had been successfully opened in a new Russian city.

So when I arrived in St. Petersburg, I was a little wary about what Urobank could do for us. But they had two key team players on this project—Richard Sloan, a thirtyish Brit, fluent in both Russian and Russia; and Paul Barron, slightly older, an ambitious and brilliant lender based in London who oversaw Urobank's Russian and Central European lending. Urobank was eager for deals, but they wanted to spread the risk of their involvement, so we were pursuing a primary lender—EXPOC—for the bulk of the funds.

To be fair, no one knew in 1994 what would happen with the development of the Russian real-estate markets. There was a sense among some, which we enthusiastically endorsed in our initial marketing efforts, that St. Petersburg could emerge as the financial capital of Russia while Moscow would remain the political capital. St. Petersburg had, after all, historically been the *window to the west*. But that was when the czars lived there. The concept of a balance between political and financial capital cities was more applicable to the United States or Germany. The better comparison would be France, where all power is concentrated in the capital city. Our bank permits were issued in Moscow, not St. Petersburg, and the amount of office space in Moscow would ultimately dwarf all other cities in the post-Soviet world.

To carry out the St. Petersburg project, our company had initiated a design/build process. We were working with a Finnish affiliate of the giant Swedish construction firm, Skanska, to selectively demolish the floors and roof of the former buildings on the site, and to replace four separate, misaligned elevations with common floors that would extend all around the central courtyard. We were also replacing the former roof with two new floors supported by steel structure, which would allow for glass walls on the upper floors. All in all, the idea was to turn the building inside out, and to make the central glass atrium the focus instead of the afterthought. This also had the benefit of creating a lot more views from the interior office spaces. Since St. Petersburg is situated so far north on the globe, the impact of white nights meant that during June and July, the sun would hit every window in the building.

Of course, in November and December there is no sun at all, only lighter and darker gray, but the long, cold winters had led to an architectural tradition of winter gardens. In St. Petersburg this was a more appropriate design feature than, say, a roof deck, which in practice would be enjoyable only about two weeks of the year. However, the word *atrium* sounded nice in English, but somehow didn't have the same pizzazz in Russian. Instead of evoking a magnificent, open central public entrance, it translated into something more like *terrarium*—a see-through container for animals or plant life. *Atrium* is actually a Latin word for an entry courtyard, well-suited to the Roman climate. Like the Italianate-style plaster-coated buildings that abounded in St. Petersburg, it would need to adapt to survive the damp and cold of northern Russia.

So demolition, or phase one, was underway, and we were spending our own money to do it. By *our money* I mean the partners' money. The main partners were Urobank (40 percent) and Neptune (40 percent). The remaining partners were Walton (9 percent) and the City of St. Petersburg (9 percent). There were two tiny shareholders as well, each holding approximately 1 percent, based on a kind of buyout, to get them to vacate the building to enable demolition. These were small commercial enterprises, and given the uncertain legal environment, it was unclear what kind of right they might have to the property where their businesses were operating. So one of the initial tasks was to reach a settlement with these businesses, whereby they received some ownership stake in exchange for vacating the premises.

While the phase-one construction work was progressing, the transition to phase two was not going well. There had been a tender, and the Finns had lost because their bid was too high. A design/build program does not produce clear milestones between the design vs. the build, or between demolition of the old vs. start of new construction, even under the best circumstances. The cultural element created an even more disjointed transition, since a Finnish company had started the project and the new contractor, Kemalco, was Turkish. I wasn't the construction expert and I hadn't been present for any of the previous battles. My role was really just to facilitate the settlement so that it was agreeable politically to all of the parties. Our experts, like Harry Marin, told me what needed to happen correctly from a technical perspective.

Sitting at the table during the negotiations was nevertheless a priceless experience. The Finns thought we owed them money for work they had done. We thought they owed us work that was incomplete. Finns tend to be laconic—*yes* or *no, five* or *ten*—and to the point. They mean what they say, exactly as they said it. Turks, on the other hand, tend to talk a lot. They are sincere, but the words are more about building a relationship and less about what is actually said. Their first-choice solution to problems was often to suggest we go out to dinner.

On their part, Russians can be quite formal. The translator hired by Skanska to translate from Finnish to Russian was very dramatic, almost as if he were auditioning for a play. He would deliver the words with wild hand gestures to convey their full meaning. At one point, Kleptov turned away from his Finnish counterpart and spoke directly to the translator. "I don't care what he said," Kleptov declared, "but *you* are a translator and I am a director and *you* cannot speak to me in that way."

CHAPTER 2

THE BANK PERMITS

On the finance side, by 1995 the initial equity the partners had invested in the company was running out and the anticipated loans were not yet available. We needed to find a way to inject more capital in order to finish the demolition and continue with the other predevelopment work in finance, design, and marketing. In the United States, predevelopment work is typically funded by developer's equity, but bank funding is used for actual construction. It is rare to start construction without all of the equity and loan funding in place. I liken it to keeping a boat safe at the dock until you have enough gas to cross the lake. If you are betting on refueling halfway across the lake, you're taking an unnecessary risk. But if you looked at many individual houses in areas that didn't have mortgage financing, like Eastern Europe at that time, you saw nothing but partially built homes, some already occupied. People built when they had money and stopped when they ran out. In a high-inflation environment or one where banks were unstable, it might even make sense.

And we were in an unstable environment. Russia had nearly 3,000 commercial banks in 1995, far more than similarly sized countries in established western markets. One result of this quantity and the newness and smallness of many of the banks was that it was never clear how stable any particular bank actually was. Less than two months after I arrived, the small Russian bank that had issued our $1 million certificate of deposit went belly up. So much for our working capital reserves.

Our partner, the City of St. Petersburg, held considerable amounts of its own deposits in the same bank. When I asked our Russian partners how they had picked the bank, they said, "Well, we figured it would be safe because the city had a lot of its own money there." My company in Chicago was livid, and pushed me to find out as much as I could.

"That money is in someone's pocket!" came the consensus opinion from Chicago in an angry conference call. "You've got to get tough. Develop a real attitude."

"I don't think so," I responded carefully.

The existence of the CD and its location in that particular bank, Nevabank, along with the rates and terms, had been recorded in official company minutes. The interest rate was the same as other banks'—not much higher, as if the company had sought risky profits, or much lower, as if someone on our side had agreed to unfavorable terms in exchange for some personal payoff. No evidence of any of that. Our Russian accountant, Maya, and Kleptov himself went out of their ways to show me everything they had about the CD. The accountant was organized and competent. I checked it out as best I could with our local Urobank partner, Richard Sloan, the young Brit who spoke Russian fluently and had been involved with the project from the start. He had the same reaction. It really looked like the whole bank went belly up, not just our CD. Our money was simply stuck in there along with everyone else's, including the city's.

But that made it more pressing to activate our next phase of funding. We weren't far enough along with the project to tap a formal construction loan/mortgage from a third-party lender, so we would have to raise more money from the partners. It couldn't, however, be in the form of equity. That would mean reorganizing the shareholdings and the company documents, re-recording and so on in all the proper places. It would also mean that future returns could only come back in the form of dividends or capital appreciation. Another benefit of using partner loans was that future returns could flow back to the partners in the form of interest or loan repayments rather than as dividends on their equity investments. Like so many other aspects of the deal, it simply wasn't clear in 1995 what the best option would be, so we created multiple options to provide backup solutions for any changing circumstances. Who knew what the tax laws or treaties between the countries would be in a few years? We did not predict anything like the future financial crises.

However, for a Russian firm to take on a loan in foreign currency, even or especially from its own shareholders, it needed permission from the Moscow Narodny Bank, or Russian Central Bank. Thus began the saga of the Central Bank permits. It was understood that it would be hard to borrow money in Russia. As it turned out, the Atrium was one of the first real-estate projects to secure mortgage-backed financing. The lender was EXPOC, the Export Opportunities Corporation, created by the US government. What wasn't clear at the time was how difficult it would become for us to borrow even our own partner money essentially from ourselves. In Russia, everything requires permission.

Our first step was meeting with St. Petersburg banks to see if we could deposit funds in US dollars as collateral and then borrow an equal amount from the local bank. As it turned out, several of the stronger international banks, like BNP/Dresdner where we had deposits, were simply not interested in taking on this type of so-called risky lending. BNP/Dresdner was a funny mix of a bank, a stew made of French, German, and Russian ingredients that combined the different personalities in such a way as to create an extreme sense of arrogance combined with not very much service.

"We have to be on time for our meeting," Maya, our accountant, implored me at one point. "They have agreed to see us."

"Maya," I said, "let me explain something about capitalism. We pay them. We are their customer. It is okay for us to be late if we are paying them. If they were paying us, I would hurry more."

Our second step was going to Moscow to get the permits from the Central Bank, or at least start the process. It was not just the permits themselves but the language of the permits that ultimately needed to be acceptable to our senior lenders. However, even with Urobank as a partner, we had no leverage at all with the Russian Central Bank, which acted like, well, a central bank. The bank was not about to change its documents, its work schedule, or even its official method of correspondence, which was to mail the permits via the Russian postal system rather than sending them FedEx or calling us so we could come to Moscow and pick them up in person.

All of our partners had connections somewhere, but none of our partners could move the Central Bank. Not Urobank from their Moscow office, not the City of St. Petersburg, not Neptune, our majority owner. We just had to keep knocking on various doors and politely maintaining some presence as the permits made their way through the system in Moscow. Everyone did their part.

Our whole management system was set up with a belt-and-suspenders approach. We had Western and Russian staff doubled up on almost every task. Since we just didn't know which approach was going to work, we always needed a backup plan. I had worked two years in Bulgaria, and we always did things this way. As soon as something seemed organized, I would start thinking of another way to do the same thing just in case the first idea didn't work out in the end. All anyone ever cared about were the results. Sometimes something that seemed silly would turn into something important, or a chance connection would lead to a valuable entrée to some office where you needed a response. We just kept trying, and I tried not to dismiss ideas out of hand.

⊂══╪══⊃

I was in a hurry as usual when I started up the stairs to our apartment office that day in 1996. It had been snowing or raining, I forget, but the dark hallway on the ground floor was a puddled mess. It had that distinct damp, smoky stench that meant you had entered a communal building, owned by everyone with no one in charge of cleaning it on more than an annual basis. Bruce Cockburn wrote a song about Nicaragua called "Dust and Diesel," which always comes to my mind when I think about the smells of developing countries.

I remember seeing the row of mailboxes, which were only tiny cubbyholes with small, numbered wooden doors. The doors had round holes, about two inches in diameter, that you could hook your finger through to open them. There were no locks or keys, and some of the doors had fallen halfway or all the way off, so that they lay on the wet floor wherever they had landed or been kicked to.

The only mail we ever received at the office or at our apartment were telephone bills, which came in the form of small note-sized pages. You had to shuffle the half-size scraps of paper to make sure you had them all in order so you could see what you owed. Payment was made in person at a special telephone office across town. Any business mail was sent by DHL or carried in person to a meeting. This was an American prejudice proven in the extreme here. A British colleague told me if he mailed his business correspondence—including our approval for a disbursement—from his hometown on a Friday, the bank in London would have it on Monday. To me this seemed crazy, given the significance of what was being sent. To him, my reaction was foolish since everyone in the United Kingdom could trust the mail.

So you can imagine my surprise that day, in the midst of all the climax of will-we-or-won't-we-close in the fall of 1996, when I looked down past my galoshes and there on the wet floor were two square envelopes with stamps on them from the Russian Ministry of Finance in Moscow. They were the original bank permits, just lying there where anyone could pick them up or step on them with his muddy boots. Not on purpose, as some show or statement, but with indifference or not even that, as the mailman randomly went about his or her daily life.

In that sense, the bank permits made a good metaphor for my whole experience. The permits were one of the first things I tried to get and one of the last things I actually received. Nothing could be more anticlimactic than seeing them on the dirty floor near the grimy puddles. I looked for a Tula-inspired hand towel, but there was none.

CHAPTER 3

"WE ARE THE OWNER ..."

I had been looking forward to testifying at the public meeting of the St. Petersburg property committee. It seemed a simple task to pick up one more technical approval we needed to satisfy our US lenders. The meeting would be a break from the everyday insanity of moving the project forward. It would be like being in Chicago—a routine public meeting, preprogrammed with a successful outcome. Plus, I could have fun speaking Russian in a formal setting. I went alone, not seeing the need for a translator.

The most difficult part was finding the address. The building itself was large, but I had misjudged the approximate direction when I set out walking from our office. I liked walking almost any time of year. The fresh air helped wake me up and the walks cleared my head. But unlike Chicago, built on a square grid, the roads in St. Petersburg, like many European cities, were built in circles or on angles radiating out from a central point. If you thought of the roads as perpendicular and parallel, you'd often wind up way off base and things that seemed close became far. The buildings were numbered 1, 2, 3, even 3a sometimes, so it wasn't that hard to find them. But I did miss the Chicago grid, where the same streets extend for miles, and the numbering system lets you know exactly where you are at any east/west or north/south intersection. That grid gives you a sense of familiarity even when you are far from home.

So I had a longer walk than I expected, but eventually I arrived. The Russian building reminded me of any public building—a grand old place from a prior century. Far more elegant when originally built than the Chicago city council chambers where I had once testified on behalf of our South-Side-development project, but less modern inside. Ironically, when I had testified in Chicago in the late 1980s, an official Polish visitor of some kind had been invited to observe democracy in action. I spoke for about five minutes. There was little discussion, and the agenda item, a committee vote on a preliminary designation of a blighted area to confirm its eligibility for loans or other subsidies, was readily approved.

We got up to leave, and an older council staff member pulled me and the Polish visitor aside. "If you wanna learn about democracy," he said to the man from Poland, "you gotta learn how it really works. He wouldn't even be here if he hadn't met first with his alderman." He turned to me. "Am I right? Tell him how you got here."

I smiled. It wasn't a secret or anything inappropriate. "Sure. We met with the alderman first," I said.

In Chicago there is an accepted system called aldermanic prerogative. No alderman votes for something in another alderman's ward unless the local alderman is in favor of it. Our local development group worked well—not perfectly, but supportively—with the local Irish politicians who had always carried a lot of weight in that city. We went to the alderman and explained what we were looking to do. She checked with her mentor, a state senator, and a week later we met in his office. He called his colleague in the mayor's office and told him he thought it was a good idea. We weren't surprised that our request had passed. We had made our case, technically and politically. You needed both.

I didn't explain all this to the visiting Pole. The staff member rambled on for a while about how things got done in Chicago. He had the air of someone who had been there a long time, and the Pole was charmed by his honesty and slight braggadocio. The St. Petersburg world was not so different, but what struck me about working in St. Petersburg versus Chicago was that the feudal system in St. Petersburg, at least when I was there, was made up of independent barons without a king. There was no question who was king in Chicago. Although there were conflicts, it would be unheard of for the mayor to bless a project, only to have his fire commissioner or planning commissioner take an opposing view. Not so in St. Petersburg, where the governor could announce a new Coca-Cola plant at a public ceremony and then the fire commissioner states his objections to it. Or rather, more precisely, his concerns that such a big new plant might need its own new fire station.

I was expecting a Chicago-style meeting. The City of St. Petersburg property committee was, after all, our partner in the project. Of course they would say yes.

The meeting was already in session when I arrived. I sat in the audience and waited my turn for our issue. There weren't many people there; maybe a half dozen on the panel seated above and in front of us, and maybe another dozen in small groups in the audience.

It was my turn to speak. To the American tourists I occasionally met while walking my dog in front of their hotel, I looked Russian. When outside, I wore a thick brown (Canadian) hat with ear flaps and L. L. Bean galoshes that looked like snow boots. One woman even once complimented me on my English. She couldn't conceive that an American actually lived in Russia. To this panel of post-Soviet public officials, I was clearly an American. I probably displayed that bright-eyed and bushy-tailed American look. There were no other foreigners in the room. They motioned for me to step forward, and I walked up to the podium.

I greeted the panel on behalf of our project and introduced myself as the person who had a request from our prospective lenders, "Evropesky Bank" and "Hix-Pok," the American lender. My comments were brief. The committee members were well aware of our plans to transform the historic building on Krasotsky Prospect into a modern office and retail center. The funding would come in the form of loans. The loan terms had been approved in general, but now we were working on details in preparation for the actual closing. One detail that had been raised by the US lender was that since we leased rather than owned the land under our building, we needed official approval from our landlord, the St. Petersburg property committee, in order to pledge the building to the lender. I was therefore asking for their approval as our landlord.

The committee members smiled. "What about the building next door?" one of them asked.

I was confused at first, but then remembered that we had agreed to work on the facade of the adjoining university building so that it matched our new facade and eliminated one more dilapidated plaster-and-dull-paint building. "Oh, of course," I said. "We have already completed the work for painting the adjacent facade, since it was part of the original design by the historic architect Stasov. We recognize that the building is a historical monument of a national character and we take the historic context seriously."

"No," the man replied, unimpressed. "Not that building. The one on the other side. On Krasotsky."

"The one with the giant LG billboard?" I asked.

"Yes."

"What about it? Their billboard looks like it belongs in Las Vegas. It sticks into our property—I mean, into the air space above our building—but I was told there isn't anything we can do about it."

"Can you paint that building too? It also needs painting."

I began to lose my patience. "You know, every time we do something to the outside of our building or even the sidewalk, we have to go talk to the historic committee for its approvals. We just finished a long discussion about what color the granite sidewalk should be and how tall the wainscoting should be. But our neighbor—another historic building, I am sure—decides he

wants to construct a giant billboard, into our airspace, and somehow he gets a permit for that."

Foolishly I carried on. "The owner of that billboard collects
rent for the sign, the big electric, neon Las-Vegas sign. Why don't
you ask the owner of the building to paint it himself? He could
use some of the money he collects from the sign."

The panel member smiled broadly at me like a Cheshire Cat.
"We are the owner."

I had to smile as well. What else to do? "We can decide this
question," I said, using a Russian phrase, *resheet vaproce*, that basically means the deal is done. I didn't need to say anything more.
They voted to approve the pledge.

Leaving the building, I smiled again at my own stupidity. Of
course they were the owner. The property committee owned all
of the buildings in St. Petersburg. Individuals owned only their
apartments inside. The state owned the hallways, the attics, and,
of course, the roofs.

The roof, I thought as I left the building, *that we can't touch.*
When I met later with the contractors, I told them to paint the
existing bricks on the one facade facing our building. We weren't
going to tuck-point the entire building, and we sure as hell were
not touching the edge of the roof. That would risk more claims
and this would never end. Before the demolition on our project had begun, our Russian staff had photographed the plaster
on the walls of the apartments that faced our building, so their
owners couldn't make claims later for cracked plaster that they
said we had caused. Painting a few bricks wouldn't kill us, and
there was a long Potemkin-inspired tradition of quick fixes for

appearance sake only. As I repeated many times during that project, we were not there to change the system. We just wanted to build a building.

The private landlords for our apartments were even more colorful than the official landlords for our project.

Before our son was born, my wife, Lisa, and I lived for a year in a two-room apartment with fifteen-foot ceilings that had been chopped out of a former czarist-era embassy residence. The twelve-foot-tall windows looked directly across the adjacent Neva River. At night the bright lights of passing freighters illuminated our windows on their way to Lake Ladoga under the famous raised bridges of St. Petersburg. I told friends and colleagues I could throw a softball and hit the Winter Palace. It was a magnificent location, but the faded elegance of the apartment ended abruptly when you stepped out the door and into the hallway.

That was where the public bathroom began. People, dogs, it didn't matter. There was a communal apartment adjacent to ours, the only other door on our landing. That apartment had been subdivided into multiple one-room apartments. By the time the dog owner walked out of their communal sub-hall and onto the landing, he may have felt like he was in Central Park. I was leaving one day and watched him do nothing as his tiny dog shit directly in front of our door.

"It's cold out," he said as he and the dog turned and ended their "walk." It was a small dog and a smaller piece of shit, but still.

Some of the people's habits weren't much better. One day in summer there had been a beer and music festival in the plaza in front of the Winter Palace. Lots of people. Lots of beer. No bathrooms. Not to worry.

When my wife and I returned to the main entrance of our building, the ancient doors were ajar, as usual. There was no lock. Just inside was a cavernous hall. I used to tell people it looked like it had been decorated with a grenade. The elegant plaster on the stair railings and walls was falling off in chunks, and the various layers of paint flaked off at their own random pace. It could have been a room on Disneyworld's haunted mansion ride.

That day, there were maybe five adult men pissing in the hall when we arrived. Not a little, but a lot. At least we lived on the second floor, so the doors they were pissing against were not ours. We climbed the stairs and passed their girlfriends, who were sitting on the steps smoking cigarettes while they waited. Why smoke outside in the park along the river when you can sit only yards from rivers of piss in an enclosed space? At least near Wrigley Field in Chicago they pee on the outside of the houses, not the inside. This was the low point for that apartment.

"We need a lock," I said to our landlady, Natalya Valentinova.

"Oh, it takes an agreement from all of the tenants. I need to get a petition. I need to—"

"We need a lock," I repeated. Lisa had endured a lot and was up for a challenge, but this was way over the top. When she became pregnant later, we knew we had to move, but at that time we weren't thinking of moving, just of fixing the problem at hand. "Look, how much can a combination lock cost?" I asked.

"Fifty dollars, easily!" she replied.

"Natalya," I told her, "go buy a lock and tell your neighbors the combination. We pay you $1,750 a month rent for this apartment. Get serious."

And she did. But she was an odd person. The windows of our apartment were filled with moss and plants at the bottom. The windows hadn't opened in years, but these mini-terrariums were built on purpose. "I grew up in this apartment," she told us when we first looked at it, "together with my French nanny." It was a two-room apartment, so I am not sure where the nanny slept. Maybe in France.

Once the plaster ceiling fell. A big patch, four to five feet in diameter, just left the ceiling and exploded into dust on our floor. We weren't in the apartment at the time—if I remember correctly, Lisa was back in the States—but it needed to get fixed. The cause was radiator water leaking in the apartment upstairs. I told Natalya.

"I'll have to negotiate with the neighbors," she said.

At first they denied knowing anything about it, but when radiator water leaks out of an old radiator that has fallen over, it leaves a certain mark. They agreed to pay for the repairs, and Natalya planned to make them herself with some help from friends. Try to imagine an entire city that has endured a revolution, a blockade, and the devastation of WWII, and then fifty years of home repairs where every job is completed by a relative using makeshift devices. It adds up to one big mess.

I told Natalya that the ceiling needed to be fixed before my wife returned from the United States. That gave her two weeks.

I came back early from work one day to find two men in my apartment wearing nothing but Jockey underwear and covered with plaster. Natalya was in our narrow kitchen that had once been a hallway—the bathroom was built under the stairs—and she was hovering over a big pot of boiling water with hot dogs floating in it. She had a jovial, festive air about her, and her hair was wrapped up in a bandana. She was an enormous woman, about forty or fifty years old, and she ordered about her shorter, thinner husband, who dutifully complied with her every direction.

Her husband and daughter were there as well, touching up the paint behind the plaster workers. They had constructed Dr. Seuss-like scaffolding from pine boards that had clearly been discarded from another purpose. And they were standing on this contraption, which amazingly held them. Building your own scaffolding is a useful and common skill in Russia. Scaffolding appeared in the ornate ground-floor entrance hall from time to time, so that someone could build a small fire to melt the frozen elbow joints in the water pipes that ran along the ceiling in this unheated lobby with an open doorway to the street outside. I could tell from counting the blackened edges of the pipes how often this problem has been addressed in this manner. What was not worth thinking about was how frequently people actually built fires on pine scaffolding within multifamily buildings with only one exit, located past the scaffolding.

Despite all that, it's hard for me to exaggerate how beautiful the view across the Neva River was. During our stay the city built a monument to Peter the Great, depicting him from the time when he was a young carpenter working incognito in Holland. Directly across the Neva was the campus of the university where I had studied Russian in the summer of 1981. All of this reinforced the romantic idea that we were living in the middle of an exotic story, albeit one that was, as my wife described it, "relentlessly interesting."

Once our son came into the picture, we had to move to a more hygienic place. We found another apartment that had less of a view, but still a view. We looked out our windows at one of the former palaces that was now a government office. Our building had a lock on the outside door and a small courtyard where we could park our car. We lived on the third floor, at the top of a staircase painted in bright-blue battleship paint, too high all over the world for lazy thieves to bother climbing up and breaking into. First-floor apartments—including mine in Chicago—were always broken into, but never the third-floor ones.

To be fair, a thief would need a bazooka to break into the front door of a Russian apartment. The doors are typically covered in steel plates, although occasionally—as with our entry hall—the locks are not aligned so that the enormous bolt doesn't quite line up with the hole it's supposed to go into. This entry hall was step one for getting into our apartment, which had another door with a typically intricate old-European safe key like you would expect to see in an Indiana Jones movie. The funny thing was that the fuse box—a Rube-Goldberg collection of wires of many different colors and ages—for the entire floor was located within the locked entry hall.

We once went to Finland for the weekend and returned Sunday evening to meet our neighbors from across the hall for the first time. A young couple, they were sitting in the hall with candles, smiling and talking, when we arrived. "Can we get to our fuse in your hallway?" they asked nicely. "Our power went out yesterday."

It was a real moment for me, seeing the patience and sense of humor it must take to live in Russia for your entire life without going insane. When the outside door lock on our new apartment froze shut once, locking me out of the apartment building, I didn't hesitate to pull the crow bar from my car and pop the lock so I could get inside. I wasn't going to wait ten minutes. Yet this couple waited the entire weekend. They could have done the same thing, popped the hallway lock and left us a note, but they didn't. Nor did they scream about how stupid it was to put a common-area fuse box inside a private hallway. As far as I know, they just waited.

With our new apartment we had a problem with the water. The water was too brown at times and the pressure was so low, the water barely reached our third-floor apartment. We tried lots of solutions. Our landlady bought a pump that sounded like a DC-6 airplane engine when it turned on after each flush of the toilet. We often needed to decide after using the toilet whether it was worth it to flush and wake the baby or not. Ultimately we learned that the source of the pressure problem was that a neighbor downstairs had installed a hot tub when upgrading his unit, and he had simply appropriated the water pressure meant for the upper floors.

To improve the water's purity, we hit on the idea of a filter, a screen of some kind. It could trap the brown sediments so we wouldn't see them when we opened the faucets.

"You can't change the dirty water in St. Petersburg!" our landlady yelled at me when I suggested that.

"I wouldn't dream of changing it," I said. "I just want a filter, so the filth stays on one side and I can live on the other."

CHAPTER 4

LYUBA AND TATIANA

So how did our Russian friends deal with this daily nonsense in their lives? Like anywhere else in the world, they escaped the city, going to their dachas on the weekends.

My most fond dacha memory is of walking out of our friends' log-cabin sauna, or *banya*, sweating and buck naked, except for the flip-flops on my feet. The temperature outside was maybe twenty degrees Fahrenheit, and a wealth of stars filled the black sky over the clearing in front of their dacha. The *banya* was built into the first floor of the guest cabin, where we were staying for the weekend. The funny thing was that when I went outside, so long as I kept my flip-flops on, I wasn't cold. My body retained the intense heat of the *banya*. Maybe something about stopping the ground from conducting the cold. It seemed silly, but it was true, and it wasn't any more ridiculous than other aspects of life there.

I reached for the bucket in the snow and threw it down into the round stone well. The bucket had a heavy lead weight locked around its handle to break the layer of ice below. After the bucket filled, I eagerly pulled it up, lifted it over my head, and poured the water over my body. Staring up at the stars, I felt every care in the world, every permit, every guard, every lender, every lawyer, flow off my body and into the snow at my feet. The icy, clean air roared in and out of my lungs as I hopped up and down on the snow. It was an incredible and unforgettable feeling that I could savor for only a half a minute before moving quickly on my flip-flops back to the warmth of the *banya* to start another cycle.

Lisa and I met some amazing people in Russia, but none were more special to us than Lyuba and her family. Lyuba looked after Charlie and helped my wife make her way through day-to-day life in St. Petersburg. We had become friends with Lyuba's family, including her husband Lev, who ran several small stores, and her completely enchanting daughter Tatiana, who sometimes worked as a translator and fixer for Lisa as she pulled together freelance articles for US newspapers. Lyuba spoke only a bit of English, but she easily made herself understood.

Our six-month-old son, Charlie, would scream when he heard Lyuba's voice, accompanied by the noise of her closing our steel apartment door, when she came by in the morning. The look in his eyes was one of pure joy.

"What are we going to do today?" she would ask in Russian, coming into the living/dining room. "We're going on a walk, going to play, going to eat." She would move her hands in front of him, acting out the various proposed activities. In Russian, all of these words rhyme—*gulyat, igrat, kushat.* Charlie simply loved it.

As a babysitter, Lyuba was All World. She also was a great friend and guide for our family, helping us to sort out the ways of the St. Petersburg world. One thing she introduced us to was the *meister* shop. If you brought in anything that was broken, they would think for a minute and then propose a solution. Collapsed stroller? Fixed and made permanently open using wooden broomstick poles cut to order and then screwed into place. And so on. Living in Russia required careful planning. The growing season, for example, was short, so all of the seeds for the summer vegetables were planted in yogurt cups and placed on window sills in the city apartment in spring before being transplanted to the dacha garden in summer.

Lyuba had short blonde hair and, like many Russian women, seemed too young to have a grown daughter. More like an aunt than a mother, she exuded a childlike manner and seemed unaffected by so much of the nonsense. She was quite good at getting through situations and didn't mind laughing at herself or anyone else. Once I was driving her car on a typical country road from St. Petersburg to the dacha and I asked her what the speed limit was.

"It's ninety kilometers an hour on this road," she answered as a cop moved out of the tall grass, "except for here, where it's fifty. That's why he's motioning to us."

I had been asking about the specific speed limit where we were, but what could I do except smile and raise my eyes skyward as I downshifted and we stopped to talk to the cop.

Lyuba was out of the passenger door immediately, smiling and walking right up to him. In the countryside, outside of the city where life slowed down, the local traffic cops could actually be quite pleasant. "Here is his license," she said. "He's an American but he speaks Russian, and he loves Russia! And look, look here at the license. He has a Class D license which is the best kind! He is a very good driver."

She was waving my DC driver's license, which I had gotten after moving back to the States. The Class D notation on the rear said in tiny letters that it was for "vehicles for non-commercial use," but apparently in Russia a *D* meant something more significant. The international driver's license that I had carried earlier when I lived in Russia had expired, so I wasn't going to show him that. All that license really did was provide a translation for name, address, etc., but for some reason it was treated as an official document. Probably because it had an actual stamped seal on it. Russians love stamped seals, especially round stamps that somehow denote a higher level of authority than square stamps.

In Russia, roadside traffic cops set the levels of fines at their own discretion, and by law they are paid in cash on the spot. There is no return for a court date and no address to mail in the payment. They are the modern evolution of a system of living off the land that has been well documented since czarist times. When I wasn't in the mood, they got under my skin, but overall they were just a small part of daily life.

Lyuba pointed to me, said something else—perhaps thank you—to the cop, put fifty rubles ($10) into his hand, and walked back to the car. He was just a young cop and acted like he didn't know what else he could have done. He simply shrugged and put the money in his pocket as I restarted the car and drove on.

Lyuba's beautiful daughter Tatiana captivated every Western man who met her. Now married with her own sons, I would bet she still does. Many Russian women are beautiful. There is something about their eyes, a slight pull at the corners, to remind you that this blonde girl in fact comes from a country that is very much a part of Asia. Tatiana was extremely bright and spoke fluent English with a faint and charming British accent, the result of the excellent schooling her father had managed to secure for her. My wife first met her when she was recommended by a fellow journalist to translate one of Lisa's freelance assignments. Tatiana introduced us to her family, and this led to her mother Lyuba looking after Charlie. Tatiana clearly understood the attention she attracted. She once said something to me about women needing to be attractive. When I responded that some men try to be attractive as well, she gave me a frown and a puzzled look that said, "What are you talking about?"

One time my wife invited Tatiana to join her in the States on a winter vacation while I stayed in Russia. "Wear big glasses," Lisa told her, "when you go for the US visa interview. Look like a librarian or they'll reject you." Tatiana wore the glasses and a business suit, got the visa, and flew to Chicago. We wanted her to see a broad stretch of the United States, so Lisa arranged two main events—watching the Green Bay Packers play the Super Bowl on a television set up in an igloo on a front lawn in Wisconsin with her brother's cheese-head wearing neighbors; and watching the Clinton inauguration parade in Washington, DC, from the balcony of Walton's lawyers' swank offices overlooking Pennsylvania Avenue.

Lev, Tatiana's father, could be very entertaining and silly. He supervised the "work" at the dacha, such as collecting the right wild grasses to properly smoke fish on the barbeque. He was completely absorbed by their small dog, which he fed by hand. Naturally the dog was spoiled, and wouldn't eat its dinner until after its owners showed him it was okay by tasting it. The father's small jumpy dog was one thing. Tatiana's big dog was another.

Actually, Bumpy Dog was owned by Kolya, Tatiana's husband. It was a pit bull and honestly made me uncomfortable. Not because of its individual mannerisms, just because of its breed. It was light tan, and partly to allay my own misgivings I called it Bumpy Dog in the presence of our small son so that he would be more comfortable with it. Bumpy Dog was a plasticized character in the Noddy television cartoons that were produced by the BBC and available on videos to children across Europe.

As we got closer to closing on our financing for Krasotsky 23 and our project became more real, I needed to beef up Walton's local representative office. Not the project company staff, but our own Walton St. Petersburg staff. So I asked Tatiana to work in our office. That did not work out so well.

"Where did you find these relics?" she asked me. "Your office is like a time warp to the old Communist world."

People addressed one another using formal patronymics— Boris Ivanovich literally meant, Boris, son of Ivan—the office saw itself as a *kollectiv*, and the endless birthday and office parties meant that the apartment office was frequently transformed into a drinking venue and little actual work got done.

In the early days of any new job, a motivated young worker
looks for ways to make his or her mark. Something simple but
helpful. Tatiana decided to reorganize the notebooks by the fax
machine. All the drafts and formal documents for the project
were kept in those notebooks in plastic sleeves. I think they had
been organized by date by A——, but Tatiana tried to group
them by topic. A—— went ballistic. The *kollectiv* left their work
desks and assembled in the kitchen where the party table was
located. They closed the door and the whispering grew louder
and louder as each member relayed his or her intelligence on the
crimes Tatiana had committed. Too young, too pretty, overly
motivated ... Not one of us. The verdict was swift. The sentence
of silence was imposed. After about two weeks Tatiana told me
it didn't make any sense for her to be there.

❦

With help from our Russian and expat friends, Lisa and I
made our lives as normal as possible. I had always enjoyed running in the mornings and tried to do it every other day. We
brought our blue-eyed dog Griffin, an Australian shepherd, to
superstitious Russia, and he always caused quite a stir when
passersby noticed the color of his irises.

I ran along the river, over the bridges, and back in a wide,
circular route that took me past the Peter and Paul fortress. I
ran with the dog summer and winter. When the river froze solid, we ran past an intrepid crew of polar-bear swimmers. They
would chop a rectangular lane in the ice near the fortress, slowly
disrobe down to their skivvies, fold their clothes in neat piles on

the ice, and then dive in and swim a few laps in the lane they'd created. They did this all winter long.

The views along the Neva River are spectacular. In the winter, the northern sun shines straight across the horizon, hardly rising at all in the sky. But this horizontal light catches the golden spires on the churches and ignites them like a vision of hope in a Hudson River School painting. Since practically the entire city center is historic, the facades create a fabulous stage to keep track of all the stories of the czars, the Revolution of 1917, and the siege during WWII. It is impossible to miss the ubiquitous clues. "The attic of an empire," my wife called it. Late one night I was walking home past the Winter Palace. It had been snowing for some time. A winter stillness was in the air, except for the music of a sole saxophone player who was bouncing his notes off the solitary and spotlit column that stands in the middle of the immense Palace Square.

Even walking down an ordinary sidewalk I would see signs still in place from WWII saying "During artillery barrages the other side of the street is safer." Walking anywhere involved crossing canals and passing wild sculptures, like the griffins on Griboyedev Canal, or the magnificent onion dome of the Church of our Savior on Spilled Blood built on the spot where Czar Alexander II had been assassinated.

Outside the city, my favorite place was the Cottage Palace built adjacent to the extensive grounds of the Peterhof Palace. Peter's and Catherine's palaces, like Monplaisir, and various small guest houses in the landscaped gardens are wonderful museums in beautiful settings, but I always found it impossible to understand how anyone actually lived there. The Cottage Palace was like a summer estate built in Newport, Rhode Island. It was a house that the czar's family could and did live in. So it had bathrooms. It had a gym. And outside there was a statue of a small boy looking up at a second-story window. This small boy was Alexander II, and the statue was built as a gift for Alexander's mother, who had outlived her assassinated son.

Even just walking our dog was an adventure. Both of the apartments we lived in were near enough to the Neva River that we could walk the dog in the adjacent parks. To get to these parks we would walk by St. Isaac's Cathedral, one of my favorite buildings because its stone columns changed color with the seasons, absorbing the frost on winter mornings and then turning from silver-white back to a deep maroon color when warmed by the sun. *Khram, Mou Khram* (Church, My Church) it boldly said across the top. I liked it in part because I felt like we were trying to add a significant building to the landscape of the city. The Atrium was our cathedral, and I dreamed of it joining these other monuments.

Walking on, we would pass the statue of Peter the Great and Senate Square, where the Decembrists staged their revolt. I knew it more for the Senat Bar located in the basement, but in 1825 the assembled soldiers had yelled for a constitution before being put down. *"Constitutsiya! Constitutsiya!"* they yelled as one, according to the legend. I told this story to a cynical Russian friend later in Washington, who was not impressed. *"Constitutsiya?"* he said. "They probably thought she was a girl."

Still, I spent a lot of mornings walking along the banks with our dog, singing Grateful Dead songs to myself, like "Black Muddy River," or trying to figure out how to approach the day's pending meetings. I was reading *The Iliad* at the time. A ten-year siege seemed like a useful methaphor for our development project, and more than once as I got dressed to start the day, I would quietly say to myself, "First a tunic, a fine one."

Reality and work did have a way of creeping into these idyllic settings, where I could find myself totally absorbed in my own invented drama. One foggy morning I was up early, maybe six a.m., and I took the dog to the park. No one around, just some large branches that had fallen. Our dog loved to fetch sticks, and over and over I hurled alternating branches. I needed to have two, because Griffin wouldn't let go of the one in his mouth if I didn't show him another one before throwing it out into the barely lit fields. Suddenly I noticed another figure moving slowly and deliberately through the fog, coming closer and closer. So now there were only two people awake in the whole city.

"Your dog is not allowed here," the militiaman said. "He must be on a leash and cannot go in the park. This is a national monument."

How many Russian policemen does it take to screw up your morning? *Toylko odin.* Only one.

CHAPTER 5

IVAN AND RALPH

However many mindless policemen there were wandering around looking for something to check on, there were also amazing individuals whom everyone listened to and looked up to. Academician Ivan Mirsky was one such leader.

At seventy-something, he was equal in age to Ralph Walton, our Walton company founder. By venturing into real estate, hotels, and other unfamiliar free markets, Mirsky was just as much a pioneer as Ralph, who had left the familiar United States to try development in Russia. Russia is still a land of titles, and Mirsky held several. Besides being recognized as an academician, Mirsky had received some of the Communist world's highest recognitions, literally a Hero of Red Labor. Richard, our Urobank colleague, showed me an old book with a black-and-white photo of a much younger Mirsky. Founder of the Nuclear Shield it said underneath the photo. A kind of Admiral Rickover figure, he had been involved in designing the overlapping missile defense system during the Cold War. His firm, Neptune, designed the Red October submarines.

I first met him on Submarine Day at our apartment office in 1995. He was an unassuming, shorter silver-haired man followed by an entourage of midlevel managers trying to match their pace to his. I was working in my corner of that office, trying to figure out how and where to get started with my job. It was about two in the afternoon, and the staff had closed itself off in the kitchen, squashed into chairs around the party table. The table was loaded with small open-faced *buter-brody* sandwiches—butter, ham, fish—and, of course, bottles.

"Someone's birthday again?" I asked as I walked by the doorway with an armload of notebooks and my laptop.

"No, we are waiting for Mirsky," someone answered. "We must honor him on Submarine Day."

Maybe you could honor him by building our building, I thought. *He might like that.*

Don't be disrespectful, their stern but wobbly looks warned.

Mirsky liked to give orders, and people jumped when he spoke. In a classic sycophantic way, followers made a show of themselves in his presence, only to disappear later when he was out of sight. Kleptov played this game all the time. He was nervous around Mirsky, like a kid who was counting the seconds till the end of his father's lecture so he could take off with the car keys. When Mirsky wasn't present, Kleptov was lord of the office parties, playful, boisterous, and unquestionably in charge; but he shrank immediately, becoming diminished when Mirsky walked into the room.

Unfortunately, my boss, Allan James, had a similar reaction to Mirsky and treated him like an avatar of his own American

father. Allan was tall, handsome, well-dressed, overly mani-
cured, and a really good golfer. On the golf course, he played
well under pressure, but around Mirsky he always seemed uncomfortable. I could imagine Allan reliving scenes with his own
father from long ago, trying to get his attention and prove he was
good enough; and then getting angry at not receiving the recognition and respect he so strongly felt he deserved. This was a
war Mirsky never knew of, fought and finished long ago in western Pennsylvania, but in St. Petersburg the flames of that war
flared back to life visibly on Allan's face, held in check only by his
clenched teeth. *Thick Face, Black Heart* was the book Allan gave
me to help me learn the Oriental powers of quiet strength.

Allan had told me when he hired me that my goal should be
to take over his job. I remember clearly the day that happened.
Allan was furious at Mirsky for not renewing the leasing, development, and management contracts that were the whole basis
for Walton being in St. Petersburg. The Russians were toying
with him, but they were angry themselves and probably confused
about why the project was taking so long. The Russians always
had the sense that they could do it better themselves if we would
just get out of their way. They didn't hide this belief, but they
tolerated our approach because they understood that Urobank
and EXPOC financing would never come without a US partner.

Mirsky's attorney, Ivan Motin, was a plump Dickensian
character who dressed in old suits and spoke with a thick,
learned British accent. "It appears," he would say in reviewing a
document, "that we are, ahem, trying to be more royal than the
king himself!"

I never asked what that meant.

That day the attorney was pushing back at us in a primeval way. My novice analysis of Russian history was that the Russians have always pushed forward until they met some solid force. "*Vperiod!* (Forward!)" they loved to say as a concluding thought to a meeting. It seemed genetically programmed into them. Knowing a boundary was there actually helped make them more secure, almost like a child who pushes his parents until he finds the limit of his bedtime.

"The contracts are invalid," the attorney repeated. "They have, ahem, expired."

Allan began to tap his pen, looking down at the small stack of papers in front of him. He had brought with him the amendments to extend our contracts and knew he'd be in big trouble back in Chicago if he didn't bring them back signed.

"We don't see the need for these amendments," the attorney went on, looking for a reaction.

Allan had told me that silence conveyed power, but his more and more rapid and forceful tapping was making the convincing argument that he was having a nervous breakdown.

"Allan," I said quietly while searching his face, "Mr. Motin is telling us our contracts are invalid. He needs a response."

What he needs, I thought, *is a two-by-four across the forehead.* He would respect that. He would back off. He wasn't so different from the South Side Irish I had met in Chicago. But Allan's loud pen tapping was making him nervous, and he wasn't finding the boundary he was looking for. I didn't want him going back to Mirsky to tell him Allan had lost his mind.

The meeting with Motin, which was to prepare for the next day's board meeting, petered out without any resolution. The next day at the board meeting, without any warning or heads-up to me or Richard, Allan slid a thick envelope across the table to Mirsky, stood up, and walked out of the apartment office. Richard and I looked at each other. What should we do as the remaining members of the Western team? Leave with him? Stay and smooth it over? *And what the fuck is in that envelope, Allan?*

Mirsky told A—— to translate it, and we all sat around waiting while she lost her temper at getting more work after a late night of preparations and translations for this meeting. "You can't squeeze me like a lemon!" she yelled from down the hall where she sat next to her notebooks and her fax.

Finally A—— returned and handed the letter, now in Russian, to Mirsky so he could read it. Eventually I saw the English version. Allan was upset. He felt betrayed. After all we had done for them, our Russian partners weren't respecting us. *Oh, shit,* I thought, *this is not what they need to hear from the mercenaries they hired to win the war and build the building.* It sounded exactly like a letter an angry son would write on parchment to his father in some movie set in the eighteenth century, only it was delivered to a Russian who never knew his father and had nothing to do with his upbringing. Allan was gone. The January 1996 board meeting was over. Richard and I looked at each other. It was our project now.

I never read Allan's book.

I thought I had developed some credibility in Chicago with Ralph Walton, who had interviewed me and everyone else on the

European team in person. He liked working in Europe because he could be himself—more old school, more look in the eye and less bureaucratic form processing. He told me that when Mirsky and his entourage had come to Chicago for due diligence on Walton and Company, his goal was simple. "Before the week is out, it's going to be Ivan and Ralph," he said. They saw Chicago, he took them out on the town, and they went to a sauna together. Walton got the deal.

In my interview he got personal early on. "How old are you? Are you married? Do you have any kids? Do you want to have kids?" he asked. All illegal questions in the United States, but in Warsaw, where I had flown up from Bulgaria for the day, hardly out of line. "Does that make you uncomfortable, asking about kids?"

I felt he was probing, testing me to see what I was made of, more than he was actually interested in the answer. So I decided to push back. "Yes, it makes me uncomfortable."

"Why?"

"It's none of your business."

"None of my business?" he shot back, his eyebrows raised. "That's my family name on that door you walked through! Why is it none of my business if you have kids?"

"Because you aren't part of the process," I said. I actually thought it was kind of funny at the time. He didn't.

"How many jobs have you had before this one? How long in each job?"

"Two," I said. "I was five years at Beverly Local Development Company, a nonprofit group, and before that three years at the Chicago Association of Neighborhood Development Organizations. Now I've been almost two years with Shorebank in Bulgaria."

"Hmph," he said. "Stable."

The interview recovered from there. Later that afternoon he asked me to paraphrase my responses for Allan, and I retold the story without any drama and no flavor. Pure vanilla. Something like, "Well, we seem to have a different understanding of family and business, and I can understand that for Mr. Walton, Ralph, his family is his business, but we've moved on from that." Once a fight was over there wasn't much point in refighting it. Move on. Plus, I wanted the job.

So Ralph hired me and he backed me up. He had a great impact on visiting the team far away. He always said, "This project is the most important one for me." Even though our building was only 80,000 square feet and the one in Warsaw was 700,000, he said this one meant the most to him. We believed him. He said, "You don't work for me, I work for you." We believed that too. And so we worked a little harder, not wanting to let him down for placing trust in us.

Something I was doing started to build trust with our Russian partners as well. I am not sure what. I did sign some documents in advance of getting any formal go-ahead because there was some practical reason for doing so. "Mirsky noticed that," Kleptov told me, "and he appreciated it." It may be that they realized I wasn't corrupt and really did want to focus on building our building. I never knew how much they actually knew about my background. I told them I had learned to speak

Russian in Washington, DC, during the Cold War and let it go at that. Georgetown University, where I got my undergrad degree in foreign service, happens to be located in Washington, DC, but the Washington reference usually made an impression. It didn't hurt.

Mirsky's right-hand person, Slova, was an interesting counterpart. Just as I had been a Boy Scout, actually an Eagle Scout at age thirteen, I was sure Slova had been a Komsomol scout. The Boy Scout motto is *be prepared* while the Komsomol motto is *always ready*. Not so different. I got the strong sense he believed in all the patriotic Russian positions in exactly the same way I would have stood up for the American ones. Not in a naïve or shallow way, but in a deeper way, tied up in a sense of how each one of us would define ourselves and live our lives. "Don't talk to me about getting out of Russian taxes," he told me once. "I pay them." I paid them as well. I couldn't go to jail like my site manager. And I learned to speak and understand more and more Russian.

I went back and forth to meet with Motin, Slova, and Kleptov. Six weeks after the January board meeting, I FedExed the three signed contract amendments to Chicago. Touchdown. The Chicago office was pleased, but then I began to hear the Golden Boy sniping from Harry Marin. I never got that. For all of his experience, he never seemed to understand that we wore the same colored jersey and there just wasn't much point in having the defense take on the offense within the same football team.

CHAPTER 6

THE LENDERS:
EXPOC AND UROBANK

"We have the best partners in the world," Ralph Walton said in that job interview.

"Urobank?" I asked incredulously.

"Okay, they're awful."

The quick turnaround had made me smile. It was just like when publicity-hungry expats in Russia discovered my wife was a journalist. "You know," they would say, "there really aren't all the problems here that people talk about. Why, we get tremendous support from the wonderful Russian authorities who work at all of the agencies, especially the office of ..."

"My husband is a real-estate developer," Lisa would say.

"Oh. So, anyway, you know how it is ..." was always their response, before they changed the subject.

In Central Eastern Europe, Urobank had a funny relationship to real estate. They were one of the most important lenders, but they always seemed cautious. They were eager to pull other lenders in as part of their mission so that they were building a market, not just pouring money in as the sole provider. Prior to the ground-breaking ceremony for the major Polska Financial Centre in Poland, Paul Barron, the Urobank lender from London, didn't realize the microphone was already on when he commented on the local Polish custom of burying coins in the excavated hole. "That's just how my board views these projects," he said. "A big pit we throw money in."

Paul's background was in investment banking, and he was exceedingly sharp. He called me once during the middle of a business trip, where he was picking through a projection I had sent. "The number sequence is somehow wrong. Look at the percentage change from October to November in all of the expenses. Why does one line item go up by 5 percent and the other by only 2 percent?" Paul had a funny way of telegraphing his self-preservation instincts as well. He was the kind of person you should keep your eye on when bad weather was approaching. If he was stepping into the lifeboat, it wasn't a good sign.

At a senior level, and in the world of banking issues, Paul was in command. On Russia-related issues, he relied on the local staff and was clearly uncomfortable with stepping out from behind the Oz curtain. Local staff meant Richard Sloan, who over the years became more Russian than the Russians, but always with a carefree approach, like some F. Scott Fitzgerald character. Richard owned two cars, a Range Rover and the Aston Martin sports car he'd brought over so he could cruise up and down Krasotsky Prospect. There wasn't really any other road in Russia that such a low-riding car could use. The ever-present Ladas, for example, had high suspension to allow them to traverse the deep potholes in summer and the ice and snow in the winter. Somehow Richard had been issued an official St. Petersburg ID card of some kind that came in a red leather case. This card basically let him ignore local traffic laws and park at will. His apartment also had a baby grand piano in it, which he might even have known how to play. I don't remember ever hearing him play it, but it seemed to have been in use. And he was single. Aggressively so, with a steady Russian girlfriend of several years who was nevertheless always kept at a healthy distance from anything like an engagement ring.

Urobank had managed the creation of the Krasotsky 23 company and supervised hundreds of thousands of dollars of legal due diligence before becoming a shareholder. This had included reviews of the title documents and company charters, as well as the due diligence on the land lease with the City of St. Petersburg. Nonetheless, as the project moved forward toward fruition, for some reason Urobank did not want to lend all of the remaining funds required for development. They preferred that Walton bring in a US government lender to be the senior lender. Ours was not a large project; the senior loan was in the range of $11 million. Perhaps to support their mission of leveraging their investments to broaden the investment impact, Urobank pushed for the involvement of another independent political institution in Russia. This more than doubled our degree of complexity in getting financing, but at that time there were few options and there had been no project-based financing executed in Russia.

The initial team from EXPOC included senior legal people, but when the details were to be negotiated, they relied on a young loan officer, Ted E——. He was glad to have the comfort level of Urobank's presence, but was not senior enough to appreciate that Urobank was running circles around him on minute details. He had a funny way of laughing at his own jokes and cocking his head to the left as he did so. Ultimately we decided he had an imaginary friend sitting on his shoulder. He was no match for Paul Barron. For example, after the US team had flown in to finalize the commitment letter, there was a $25,000 fee associated with the letter. At the last minute, Paul said, "I don't want the company to have to pay the fee. Not just yet." That abruptly ended the smiles and changed the dynamic of the conversation. Suddenly EXPOC was pushing for the financing to go through, and Urobank, as a board member for Krasotsky 23, was acting cautious. I later saw Ralph do the exact same thing to one of their corporate funders, hesitating to fund the company's 10 percent match after convincing the main lender to advance their 90 percent loan. The funder's reaction was similar—total disbelief at first, but then acquiescence.

Two sets of lenders meant four sets of legal conversations, as well as a complete repeat of the due-diligence process on the company documents and leases, etc. Urobank's legal team was based in Moscow and didn't get too involved in the process. But the EXPOC legal team was large and costly and seemed to want to verify everything, to the point of asking us to contact the original small retail tenants who had been more or less evicted from the dilapidated building prior to demolition on the promise of small shares of stock—1 percent each—in the new building once it was completed.

"We see that they promised that their rights have been transferred," one attorney told me, "but it would be stronger in English if we could get these people to re-sign a new agreement saying that they not only promise but also *undertake* that they have transferred their rights."

"Are you kidding?" I asked. "These people don't speak English. They made a deal once and now they're gone and this issue is buried. Undertaking? Like something dead? It sounds to me like you want to go back into the cemetery, dig this agreement back up, and tell someone you've never met that they need to re-sign their agreement—but that the new agreement isn't really any different from their former agreement, so they shouldn't get anything new for their troubles. Don't you see that they wouldn't trust that approach? At the very least, they'll ask for something else before they'll agree again to what they've already agreed to."

"Well, I promised our boss in DC we would try to insert that one word, and he thought it was a good compromise to give us more security."

"Does he speak any Russian?"

"No."

"Let's leave it alone for now, please," I said. "I don't even know where to find these people and I'm afraid to ask."

My role in the initial negotiations was limited. Walton had a director of finance in Chicago, Roger Glass. He and Allan had been meeting with the lenders in Washington and working with Paul in London. I was supposed to tackle the partner loans locally and navigate the Russian regulations. Still, at times initially it grated on my nerves.

During one marathon session in St. Petersburg, we met with the EXPOC attorneys in our cramped apartment office, where our staff served imported paprika potato chips along with instant coffee. A perfect way to maintain my stomach's composure. Russians weren't used to drinking coffee at that time. They would usually serve elaborate or at least well-made tea for themselves, but the instant coffee for Westerners was never quite right. However, there was also a large bowl of cookies, which the EXPOC lawyer, Jack L., latched onto immediately. We went through page after page of edits with our attorney, Greg G. When we took a break, Greg pulled me aside.

"Do you know the stores around here?" he asked.

"Sure," I answered.

"Good. Go get some more of these cookies. We're running out."

Half-teasing, and a little pissed off, I said, "Hey, I've got an MBA from the University of Chicago."

"So what?" he said. "We don't need that right now. Right now we need some cookies. Have you noticed that as long as Jack's munching on the cookies, he agrees with every suggestion we make. Now they're almost gone. I'm not risking going through the rest of the agreement without the cookies."

I left to get the cookies.

Greg was extremely smart and could actually be quite funny in a deadpan way. His greatest thrill of the entire project was one time on the site when he noticed a forklift with the brand name Putzmeister. "Oh, yes," he said, "I need a photo of myself here in front of this!" Our meetings usually ended with an obligatory banquet dinner at Kleptov's favorite Krasotsky restaurant, where they had a show revue like you might find in Las Vegas. After one routine with scantily clad dancers, Greg looked down at his glass bowl with two large round scoops of vanilla ice cream in it. "I think I have déjà vu," he said.

When it was just the expat crowd going out, we tended to skip the Krasotsky revue, but the hotel restaurants could be pricey. Chopsticks, the Chinese restaurant at the Grand Hotel Europe, struck me as the most expensive Chinese restaurant on the planet. After a difficult session involving all the attorneys for Urobank and EXPOC, Paul suggested dinner at Chopsticks to unwind. He assumed the seat at the head of the table. Taking a menu in one hand, he waved the other arm grandly above his head. "I'll order for the whole table," he said. "We'll have several of the lamb, and oh, yes, some of this and a lot of that." The young EXPOC attorneys were nervous but glad to be taken care of in the company of the whole crowd. At the end of the meal for twenty, Paul took the check and handed it to the youngest attorney. "Our tradition," he said. "We always give the bill to the youngest lawyer." The young man looked stunned. "C'mon," Paul said. "You know you're going to expense it anyway to the client, and that's us." Relieved, the young man took out his credit card.

The legal bills became less funny over time. The due diligence was endless and the sense of actual loan agreements was far away. The Russian partners began to lose patience with ever more documents, and right up to the closing they would shout and say, "No more, we're not translating or signing anything more." So I made bets I knew I would lose, telling them each time that I'd buy a bottle of whiskey if there are any more documents, but I needed them to review this one so we could send it back. These documents were things like share pledges, security documents, other pledges and requirements that made no sense to the Russian partners, like earthquake insurance. "We don't have earthquakes in this geological zone," the Russian engineers told me as if I were a student.

"We need the insurance because the consultant for EXPOC is based in San Francisco," I said, "and he won't approve the loan without this type of insurance."

My Russian colleague paused for a minute. "Okay, we get it," he said. "You have a share of the insurance bill. That's fine. You don't ask for much."

"No, I do not have a slice of the insurance commission," I tried to explain.

I actually hated the insurance discussion, because calling San Francisco from St. Petersburg meant I was literally lying on the floor of my apartment because I was so tired, calling at about 10 p.m. our time, which was when the office in San Francisco was open. For the construction contract, we needed insurance with *nonvitiation*.

"What?" the Turks from Kemalco asked when I told them. "We don't have that in Turkey."

"We need it, so let's find a way," I said.

"Let's go to dinner and discuss it," they said.

But the months were passing and the loan was still not in hand. Some delays seemed ludicrous to the Russian partners.

"We won't receive the draft this week," I told them once, "because it snowed in Washington, DC, last week and our federal government is closed."

The look on Mirsky's face was priceless. "This is a superpower?" he said. "What is the real reason? Why don't you tell us?"

Meanwhile the estimates of the construction costs were increasing and the legal bills kept mounting. And the partners had other ideas on how best to spend the budget.

"The atrium itself is not grand enough in the current design," Mirsky said at one board meeting. "We need something more fitting."

The Russian architect, Soska, came back several weeks later with elegant designs for inlaid granite patterns and a central fountain in the middle of the space.

"We don't have any money for a fountain," we complained, and besides, the liability insurance for slips and falls would need to be $1 million. We have a US developer and a US lender....

"A million dollars?" they asked. "There are things about your country we cannot understand at all. If a worker dies here, the family will get approximately $5,000 and that will be enough if the person is *dead*. One million dollars for slipping and falling?"

"That's how our country works."

"These laws do not beautify your country," Mirsky said slowly and deliberately, shaking his head.

One board meeting was nearly a disaster. As a type of value engineering, the US team suggested that since the budget was tightening, we could take a new approach to the atrium design. "Let's put in ceramic tiles on a temporary basis," we suggested, "until the building is fully leased. Then we can replace the ceramic tiles with granite later when we have more money." To a man, the Russian partners went crazy and started talking wildly to one another. Mirsky waved his hands and shook his head no.

"There are temporary buildings still in use here that were built in 1945." The room fell silent. *"Nichevo tak postayana kak vremena,"* he concluded. Nothing is more permanent than temporary.

The meeting adjourned without a solution. Mirsky was upset when he left, muttering to his colleague on his way out the door, "I will not lose my face in this city."

So we began to plan for the next board meeting. I met privately with all of the partners and eventually reported back to Walton that the Russian partners weren't kidding about the fountain, or the legal bills.

"We won't pay them," our Russian partners said. "The hell with the lawyers."

"But these are lender's legal bills," I said. "If we don't pay them, the lenders will just look at us and they certainly won't give us the loans."

"We'll never get the loans anyway. And, *no*, we don't want to bet you another bottle of whiskey. We appreciate what you are doing, but the answer is no."

So I called my Walton team in Chicago and then met with Richard Sloan and told him my best idea on how to handle the next meeting. "First they are going to talk about the fountain,"

I said, "and how necessary it is for the beauty and pride of the building. When they bring this up, please tell them it is a good idea. Then they will mention the legal bills, and they will tell Walton that we did not do a good job as the developer managing the lawyers. They will express shock at the size of the bills and the need to quickly close the loan. We will apologize and say we'll monitor the lawyers more closely, and then they will approve the legal bills and we'll be done with it."

"Okay," Richard said, "but let's see the design of the fountain. I think it might be better if—"

"No, no, no," I said. "Richard, please play your position on the field. We do not have an opinion on the color or the shape of the fountain. It's their thing. It will cost us about $50,000. Let's just let them have it and they'll pay our $300,000 legal bills. Please."

The meeting flowed like a well-conducted symphony, but we were still not close to closing the loan. Another aspect needed to be cleared up, related to the financial management of the company. Urobank wanted the Russian partners to take some responsibility for the loss of the $1 million CD, and they wanted to give some assurances to EXPOC that there would be a strong American presence in managing the loan. A compromise was agreed upon prior to the meeting, whereby Grigory Kleptov would be demoted to assistant director and I would be promoted to general director. Kleptov would take responsibility for the loss of the CD. Paul Barron understood that this would all be handled in due course, but Mirsky had no intention of taking sole responsibility for the decision of all of the partners.

So at the end of the meeting, Mirsky said there was still one more matter. Kleptov looked genuinely confused and nervous as the conversation began. He could see he was being set up for a fall.

"I hate being here for this," Paul said. "Chairman Mirsky, can I be excused? I'm feeling sick ..."

Mirsky glared at him and then said softly, "Paul, I have been sick for ten years. No, you are not excused." Mirsky then stated that Kleptov would need to take responsibility for the loss of the funds that had occurred on his watch, and they nominated and approved me as general director. It was over in ten minutes.

"You will meet with Grigory and make arrangements on how to transfer responsibilities," Mirsky said to me.

Kleptov and I met the following Saturday. "Please, please," he said, "I would really like to keep the green BMW. Everyone knows it is my car and if I lose it everyone will know that I have lost my position."

I didn't care about the car. I walked to work and spent my whole day in the office. Plus, he needed it for liaison meetings. "The car is fine," I said, "but the private office will be mine."

The private office was the source of half of our distractions, and it was the only private room in the whole apartment office. Besides being a symbol of my actually becoming general director, it would terminate a lot of silliness. Kleptov wouldn't be meeting many people in our open-plan office area where I had sat as assistant director.

So we pushed forward with the loan documents and the permits and the various other items. The final initiative to push for our closing was actually something juvenile and competitive on my side. Our Walton St. Petersburg team had been invited to the groundbreaking for the Polska Financial Centre.

"It's too bad you're not ready yet, but this will be a nice event," our senior Warsaw colleagues told us.

"Not a chance," I told my coworkers. "We are not going to a pity party in Poland to listen to the other team tell us about their project. Let's make sure we close too."

But our Walton team in the States hesitated over some of the final details. Allan and Greg flew to St. Petersburg, but didn't seem convinced we were ready to close. One day as Allan and I walked down Krasotsky Prospect to get some lunch, Allan said I was too eager, that I didn't understand the more cynical calculations that had to be made a higher level. "I worry about you," he said. "I worry what happens to you when you lose all of your enthusiasm."

"Okay," I said, "let's count together. If Walton closes, we need to fund another $500,000 in partner loans. The Krasotsky company owes Walton about $150,000 now, and they owe Greg nearly a hundred as well. If we don't start building, we get no more development fees. For managing construction, we'll earn another $500,000 in development fees, plus the chance to earn a lot more in leasing fees. What 'higher-level' math am I missing?"

Eventually, with a little luck and more perseverance, we did close. One night in November 1996, at dinner in the same Indian restaurant where I had come for my first visit to St. Petersburg in 1995, Richard Sloan handed me his latest cell phone so I could speak to Allan and hear the news firsthand. Walton and the banks had wired their funds. Now we really could build the building.

New construction in front of St. Isaac's
illuminated by the winter sun.

Scaffolding next to the interior façades. A grand stage.

CHAPTER 7

BUILDING A GLASS HOUSE

"People who live in glass houses shouldn't throw stones."

"Now all you have to do is build it!" My older brother, Greg, an engineer by training who has been in construction all his life, hates hearing these words. From a developer's point of view, though, there is something lighthearted about the start of construction after so many stops and starts with the financing, permits, and preparation. It does seem almost done before you start at that point.

In August and September of 1996, we were blessed with three weeks of no rain in St. Petersburg. We had wanted to get a jump on the facade work to make a marketing statement. We didn't have all the permits or all of the money yet, but if we could show the city—and potential tenants—that we had broken ground, so to speak, we could gain a lot more credibility in the market. A little bit of a game, played all over the world, but we found ourselves playing even as we were being played.

To get the contractor on site for the early start, we had to agree to pay for their mobilization and overhead. Eighty thousand dollars a month for three months. More at-risk money from the partners before Urobank and EXPOC loans were closed, but worth it if we could get the results and the public-image boost for our long-stalled project. Our incremental progress with the lenders and the permits was evident to us, at least on the American side, but invisible to the market, city politicians, and our Russian partners. Work on-site had been on hiatus since the spring, when the demolition and stabilization was completed. Even though we had signed the general contractor contract in April, we had not issued their notice to proceed, since we hadn't closed the loans that would give us all the money to pay them.

The signing of the Kemalco construction contract back in April had been a nice morale boost. We had made this minor event part of Urobank's annual meeting, held that year in Sofia, Bulgaria. The Russian partners were very excited about the trip. They nominated me as *starshe*, which I thought meant senior guide because I had lived there before, but it turned out to be more like designated driver for spring break. My wife came with us on the trip. The Russians took us to the local pole-dancing bar, located in the basement of the Park Hotel Moskva, which ironically was only a few blocks from where Lisa and I had lived in Sofia. Somehow, we had never made it to the pole-dancing bar when we lived nearby.

We signed the Kemalco contract early in the morning at our breakfast table in the restaurant of the Park Hotel. "Don't take photos now," Kleptov warned. "If people see we were drinking only orange juice, no one will believe this was a serious contract."

Work by our Turkish contractor on the most modern high-tech office building in St. Petersburg began in an old-fashioned, low-tech way with their Russian subcontractor. Rickety and filthy scaffolding was soon erected across the old facade, and a brigade of heavyset women arrived with buckets of plaster in one hand and wire scrub brushes in the other. It could easily have been 1939 or 1814. Dressed in layers of faded powder blue, they climbed the scaffolding and opened fire. From a distance of one to two yards they hurled plaster at the bricks in a time-honored technique for encouraging the new layer to adhere to the old. I don't remember if they were actually singing or if I dreamed up that part from a movie, but in my memory they were. It was as if the word had gone out to Tula and the Motherland had answered.

Dozens and dozens of them worked feverishly while foremen paced. And then Mirsky arrived with another car of his staff. Kleptov greeted him at the curb and proudly pointed at the buzz above. Mirsky only stayed about twenty minutes, enough to greet the Russian subcontractor and walk back and forth before gathering up his staff from Neptune and departing.

This was just before lunch. I left for my own lunch and to go to the bank to get some dollars to pay my monthly rent. The process of withdrawing money took about half an hour, going from window to window inside the ancient, dusty bank. When I walked back down Krasotsky Prospect an hour and a half later, I was confused. There was silence. The scaffolding was still there, of course, and bits of gray sludge had been splattered across the bricks wherever one of the women had been standing. But the buckets themselves were gone. So were the people. Gone.

As it turned out, the Potemkin brigade had been called to another job. We called Kemalco. We were told that the sub-contractor had informed them that he had a crisis on another job site. As soon as it was resolved, they would be back. So we waited. And waited. Nothing. We counted the number of work-ers on-site each day. Six, four ... none. Two months passed by, $160,000 in fees for mobilization, and one of the warmest, driest Septembers that St. Petersburg had ever seen. Kleptov said he was working on it, and we discussed it ad nauseam at each week-ly meeting, but I was consumed with the financing work and other nonconstruction tasks, and it really bothered me because I knew I had been had. Worse, I had pushed our company to agree to the $80,000 per month, and I looked naïve and foolish to my own bosses back in Chicago, not to mention Harry Marin. Still, we paid the money. We had agreed to the terms, so we hon-ored them. But I wouldn't forget; and as my Chicago friends say, "What goes around, comes around."

"My word is my bond," Kemalco's senior construction man-ager Ghilal told us. We wanted something else. The facade ep-isode had gotten us off on the wrong foot with our contractor, but once actual construction was underway, we were much more focused on trying to keep the contractor to the schedule. The lenders would insist. Still, the Turks were hard to pin down.

"We respect all cultures," they would say. "In Russia we drink vodka because the Koran says nothing about it. We know that we can't drink beer or wine."

The Turks did work hard. Once we gave them the actual notice to proceed, they brought in about a hundred workers to live in trailers and dormitories, and they took the whole project more seriously. However, we needed to keep a close eye on the weekly progress. We got a big help in this from Nigel H., the lender supervisor sent in to represent Urobank and EXPOC. It is always useful to have such a person around, but Nigel was world-class and well suited to the job. He was a former British army sergeant who seemed to have a hollow wooden leg and could drink Kleptov under the table. The Russians had thought they could deal with him as they would any foreigner, but late into our first dinner I watched Kleptov's head begin nodding in slow, circular motions while Nigel sat up straight, smiling and focused, his chin on his hands like he was at a chess tournament. Nigel would arrive Monday afternoons, spend three days at our site, and then fly back to London so he could take his daughters to school on Fridays. He did this all over the world—Kazakhstan, South Africa, anywhere—with just the same routine. Always propping up the photo of his kids in his hotel room and making sure that whatever crisis was at hand, he would solve it by Thursday evening.

At Krasotsky 23, Nigel started in on the Turkish scaffolding. "I represent EXPOC and that scaffolding is not up to OSHA standards," he said.

"It is very safe," Ghilal assured us with confidence. "I checked it myself. And what is OSHA? We are in Russia."

"Have it your way," Nigel responded. "Let's check to see if your scaffolding complies with Russian law first."

"We are building the building exactly in full compliance with SNIP," Ghilal declared, using the name for the Russian construction standards—*Stroitelnie Normi I Praktiki.*

Martin, Kleptov's assistant, was stunned. "No one can comply completely with SNIP," he told Nigel with a look of confusion. "The rules are contradictory. Everyone knows that."

"Right," said Nigel. "I thought I had the right man for the job. Go home tonight, Martin, and find everything about the scaffolding that doesn't comply with SNIP." The next day Nigel presented Ghilal the many pages Martin had assembled. We didn't hear any more about SNIP.

Nigel had a hard job trying to bring Western standards to Russian norms, and it made for many quizzical reactions on both sides. Take asbestos. Asbestos-laced cement was a staple of Russian construction. It was called for in the design of the protective barrier for the gas pipe that would run across the neighboring university property to bring gas to our building. Kleptov had been so excited to get this design approved, and he didn't want to change the slightest detail and risk reopening the whole issue. Nigel wouldn't allow it.

"Urobank will not fund asbestos in the construction. Period."

"How else would you do it?" the Turks and Russians asked.

Sometimes there wasn't a right answer. Take fire safety. The Russian rules were written so that the structure of the building was protected, say by layers of fireproofing materials on the steel. The Western practice was different. By Western standards, it would not be a tragedy if the roof collapsed in a fire, because that would allow the smoke to escape and thereby provide more of a chance for people in the building to escape. Smoke was what killed people in a fire, and the people were the most important consideration. This came up in Warsaw as well, in a related context, in the Class A high-rise office Walton was developing.

"Where are the fire-fighting tools for the tenants to use?" asked the Polish fire marshal.

"What?" said our development people.

"How will the tenants fight the fire without tools in the hallways?"

"The tenants won't fight the fire," our colleagues answered. "They will run out of the building! These are lawyers and accountants and they are our tenants. What are you talking about?"

Still, construction moved on as it does for any building, with a healthy amount of fighting between the architects, consultants, contractors, and owner over what the designs actually said and how best to interpret the intent of the drawings. In Russia, the design is more of a guideline, while what would be called shop drawings in the West are actually the legal controlling documents. In the West the architect's design controls, and the shop drawings are more of a confirmation that the contractor understood what the architect designed. Like many things in Russia, the relationship between the architect and the contractor seemed upside down—to both sides.

In early April 1997, we had had another big fight about change orders and whose fault it was. As usual, it ended with a dinner. We always resolved everything at a board meeting and then went out to dinner. When Kleptov was general director, we had these dinners at the Krasotsky Restaurant, which was Kleptov's favorite hangout. Going out for a business dinner then wasn't simple. It involved issuing a guaranty letter from our company and all sorts of negotiations that kept Kleptov busy for at least half a day. That wasn't my system. I just told the secretary to call and make reservations, and I'd pay with the company credit card. The Russian economy was evolving every year, and I didn't have time for the complicated payment discussions. It shouldn't be that complicated to pay for dinner at a restaurant. I didn't need a kickback.

Since the restaurant was next to my apartment, I stopped by before the scheduled dinner to make sure everything would be okay. The Adamant had small rooms and we would have about fifteen people all at one table.

"I would like Russian hospitality," I told the maître d'. "No empty glasses." He promised to make sure there were enough waiters at our table to refill any shot glasses. Americans in Russia loved the vodka mystique—even today, sports commercials are filled with Ketel One parties—but Russians never drink vodka on an empty stomach. There is no food shown in a Ketel One commercial, just guys in black ties and white shirts drinking vodka on the rocks. A Russian table always has food, such as mounds of fatty appetizers of fish, bread, cucumbers, anything that can soak up the vodka. There is a lot more common sense than meets the eye in the way that they drink.

Our group wrapped around a long U-shaped table, like in a *Godfather* movie, with the men representing the five families—the architects, Neptune as the owner, Walton as the developer,

Kemalco as the contractor, and Urobank, the lender and partner. There were only two women present: A——, the translator for Mirsky, and another translator. None of the local Russian managers would ever think to bring their spouses to an event like this, but the expats were treated differently.

"Where is your wife?" they asked me. "Didn't you say she is back in Russia now?"

Actually, she had just flown back to St. Petersburg that day, bringing with her our six-week-old son. "She just got back tonight," I said. "And she has the baby."

"Your *son!* We want to see him!"

I looked at their faces. They were sincere. I was taken aback, but called her to ask if she wanted to come with Charlie. She said yes.

When Lisa and Charlie arrived about a half hour later, they were instant celebrities. The no-empty-glasses policy had everyone in a good mood, and we had settled our latest big fight on the project, but their arrival put everyone over the top. The people with whom we had just finished heated arguments were totally overcome when they saw the baby.

"Look at this guy!" the Turkish contractor exclaimed, scooping him up. "So strong!"

Six weeks old and a Williamson baby meant he was pretty little, but they acted impressed. They passed him around the table, each one of them holding him and then handing him to the next man.

Charlie made the entire round, about thirteen people in all. Only two declined to take him. Allan, my boss, was wearing his black Hugo Boss outfit and said to me quietly but directly, "I'm afraid what your baby will do to my suit." And Richard, my worldly Urobank friend, looked completely scared. A deer in the headlights. Richard could walk into any Russian situation with carefree confidence. He once passed a convoy of armored trucks carrying minted coins, cutting in to pass them on the two-lane road as if they were regular weekend traffic. The militia reacted badly to that and pulled him over immediately. Even with the red card he carried, it took a while to calm them down. But here he was, staring at Charlie with the look of a determined single guy in his thirties that said quite clearly, "I don't know what that is. I don't want to know where it comes from or how it got here. A baby has nothing to do with me."

For me, my baby son was everything, the antidote. Holding him on a Saturday, carrying him around the apartment, bouncing him in my arms and clucking my teeth as if he were trotting on a horse. Showing him all the interesting things, like the Turkish janissaries riding in groups and hiding in the giant ceramic bowl we had bought in the bazaar in Istanbul.

Lots of people our age had families. The young Turkish manager, Mehmet, had a Finnish wife, and his family lived in St. Petersburg for a time. He'd been having difficulty going to see them in Finland, but even when they moved to the same city he was caught up in the project and experienced the work/life balance issues of anyone his age. "I am not seeing them," he told me once in a sincere way, like any young father who is working many hours to get ahead.

I liked Mehmet. He was a good guy. My wife and I did try to connect with him and his wife. We invited them over to our apartment for dinner, but either the invitation got scrambled or he couldn't work it out with his wife and kids for that night. I never figured it out. All I know is we waited for them. I even walked back to the job site, but I couldn't find him or find out where he was. We sat in our apartment at the table next to the windows, looking out on the street to see if Mehmet and his wife were coming. It was quiet. There were few cars or people on the street.

Suddenly we realized that the flags on the city administration building—the Marinsky Palace across the street—were being lowered to half-mast. We thought Yeltsin had died. Russian flags on government buildings are attached to a pole, and a fan machine blows air constantly on the flags so that they are always waving. Very Russian. We turned on the television set. Nothing. We thought we were being caught up in a dramatic moment, part of Russian history, but the next day we realized that the date was June 22. The dramatic lowering of flags was simply the annual commemoration of the invasion of Russia by the Nazis in 1941. So we were being overly dramatic, caught up in Russian fantasy tales that didn't have anything to do with our day-to-day lives.

❦

Our construction project moved on. Two months later, on August 27, Kleptov walked into our office looking ashen.

"Something terrible has happened," he said. "I just drove down Krasotsky Prospect and saw a car surrounded by policemen. I know the car from the government license plate … 005."

That Monday morning the deputy mayor of St. Petersburg, Mikhail Manevich, our partner, had been assassinated while riding in his white Volvo. He was sitting in the backseat of the car next to his wife when the bullets came through the windshield and the roof. A sniper fired six shots from a Kalashnikov, and four of the shots hit and killed Manevich. As the head of privatization in St. Petersburg, he had been involved in many transactions. For our project he was the official representative and a member of our board. I didn't know him well, but he was a friend of Richard's. Less than a week before, I had toured the Krasotsky 23 site with him and his wife to show them the progress we were making and to ask for help with paperwork. My notes from that day read "1 month registration for Bhs [British Home Stores] Lease, Opening Party plus/minus October 20."

Manevich was young, in his thirties, and his wife was absolutely lovely. He was a smart, young politician. Jewish, I believe. At his wake watching his family, I couldn't help but consider them like any middle-class immigrant Jewish family from New York City, thinking about how proud they were of their son who had done so well. Our project company was at the wake, as a normal and correct thing to do. Mirsky stood at attention for some time. It was the first time I noticed his hands shake as he held them clasped in front of him as he stared straight ahead.

People who have worked in Russia sometimes talk about the Mafia-style Wild-East experience as a kind of red badge of courage. This wasn't like that at all. There was no cash money in our project—nothing but bank transfers of closely monitored funds with dozens of attorneys and lenders and others watching everything. It wasn't an import-export business or a restaurant. There was nothing to steal, and so was of little interest to any Mafia-related business. And personal safety was never a concern. No one knew or cared who I was as I walked down the streets, which were actually quite safe at all hours in those years.

Still, we were working incredibly hard, trying to do something really special with an international partnership redeveloping this landmark building. Since I was also in my thirties, what so upset me about Manevich's murder was that a young bright person, one of the hopes of that world we were working in, had been wiped out by some scumbag. And for what? And with his wife in the car next to him. If that was the world they wanted to live in, why were we bothering? After firing his shots, the sniper had simply left the semiautomatic rifle leaning against the wall for the police to find after he walked away.

"Yes," said our company security officer, sighing. "The sniper was accurate."

I called Ralph Walton and told him the news. He asked me to set up a meeting for us to go see Mirsky. "It's not about a building," he said. "We need to find out if this is the kind of place where we can do business." He and Robert Goldman, Walton's executive vice president, flew to St. Petersburg two weeks later, on September 8.

The newspapers were filled with stories about the *Bankers War* in Moscow, where competing oligarchs were vying to secure privatizations of massive, former Soviet concerns. Some of

Yeltsin's team, who had worked together in St. Petersburg earlier, had tried to manage or change the rules between the government and the competing parties. The oligarchs fought back, and one of Yeltsin's advisers had been forced to resign as privatization chief after news was leaked that he had received a mysterious $100,000 book advance from an obscure Swiss firm. A lot of dirt was being thrown around.

We met with Mirsky. He didn't know all of the details as to who had shot Manevich or why. But he tried to assure us that this tragic event was probably part of a much larger fight that had everything to do with Moscow politics and major Russian privatizations, and nothing at all to do with small real-estate projects like our building. Ralph was shaking his head but we continued with our project.

At Manevich's funeral, which was shown on television, Prime Minister Anatoly Chubais yelled from the podium, "'We shall get them all, those who pulled the trigger and those who paid for this with their stinking stolen money. 'We shall get them all because now we have no choice. Now it is either us or them."

"Will the police arrest these people?" I asked Slova. "At least the guy who fired the gun?"

"The time is not right," he told me, "to answer these questions."

There was never a clearer moment when I realized the gulf between our two countries. Of course we had had famous assassinations in the United States—JFK, RFK, MLK—but these were followed by inquiries, arrests, trials, and then agonizing over why they had happened and who else may or may not have been involved. I couldn't imagine such an event in the United

States being understood as something that was not right to solve at the time.

⟐

So we went on with our work. In the midst of construction we decided to add a new entrance to the building on Krasotsky Prospect. In a way, it was a common-sense idea we should have realized earlier, but the original design had been for an office building, with side entrances from Kanalskaya Street. Our marketing efforts clearly showed there would be retail interest in the first-floor space, but only if we could offer a direct entrance from Krasotsky Prospect.

The building was a landmark of national significance, and there had never been a main entrance on Krasotsky. So we needed to find a historic way to create one. Soska, our architect, was well connected as the former chief architect of the city, and this was his finest hour. First, I should explain that the first floor of our building was actually the second floor of the original building, which had been constructed in 1805, prior to the raising of all the streets in St. Petersburg in order to accommodate a new sewage system. Thus, from a purist's perspective, the facade had already been altered when the street was raised. The arguments and, more importantly, the people—Soska and his colleagues— were persuasive enough that we were able to get all of the various approvals and permissions to make the change.

Internally, a staircase system would eat into the floors and require additional structural work. It was complicated and set back our completion schedule by another several months. From a development point of view, however, we had to remember why we were renovating the building in the first place—to lease it out to good tenants at the highest possible rates. The definition of a beautiful building is one that is fully leased, and in that sense we were focused on adding beauty to the building through the changes in the design. Retail leasing rates were higher than office rates, so this would be an obvious plus. However, all of the building attributes that office tenants like, such as security and quiet, are not the same attributes that retail tenants like, such as easy access and buzzing activity. Our mixed-use building would be more complicated to manage than a pure office building, but that was not our concern at the moment.

By the summer the die had been cast. We had retail tenants interested in the entire first floor and we were on a schedule to be in line with their merchandising seasons. You can't have a grand opening for a retail store in February—most insisted on the back-to-school time or Christmas. However, as the summer of 1997 drew to a close and fall approached, we were faced with more problems that threatened to derail all of these logical plans.

"Fifty Years of Nodortechnadzor" the banners proudly proclaimed. I could almost hear the people singing their eternal praise. Russians love anniversaries. Five, ten, fifteen, and especially fifty years were a big deal. I had seen the banners and read them, as I tried to read all of the various slogans left over from the Communist times, as well as announcements of coming events. One juxtaposition was classic. "Now greet Soviet Communism!"

proclaimed one rooftop sign, while the matching sign on the adjacent building said, "If you smell gas, call 311."

Kleptov and I were both still a little hung over as we walked down the sidewalk. The weekend before, Kleptov's son had married his American fiancée. They had held a nice reception at a restaurant on Krasotsky Prospect, of course. The evening had gone on merrily and ended with two vivid images. One was of Kleptov, lying on his back and held in the air on a makeshift scaffolding created by the straining arms of several of his friends, so he could sign his initials in the ceiling with a cigarette lighter. This was clearly a local tradition at the restaurant. He was merely adding his initials to the others already there. The other image kept bothering me in the back of my mind. One of my staff had walked out of the reception with a bottle of vodka for the road. Not a good sign, I thought, when you leave a Russian wedding needing another drink.

Kleptov and I were on our way up the stairs to another dingy government office. We were responding to an official letter we had just received, informing us that, basically, we were in big trouble.

"Your boiler was imported without the proper authorization," the official informed us. "You do not have a design for your boiler and your boiler has not been properly tested. It cannot be installed until it has been properly designed and tested. *Vsyo.* (That's all)."

These conversations always scrambled my brain, because I would translate the words literally as they were spoken and then they never made any sense. To me a design was only needed to guide the construction of something that had not yet been built. Our boiler was not only manufactured, it had already been installed on the fourth floor of our building, underneath the fifth floor and the roof.

"Why do we need a design for something that is already built?" I asked.

"Because you don't have one."

"Why can't we show you the plans that the Finns used to actually build it?"

"Because you need a Russian design."

"We'll translate it."

"It's not the same thing. A Russian design needs to be done by a Russian designer."

Here we go, I thought. "Okay, which Russian designers are available for this task?"

"As a matter of fact, we have an affiliated private design firm that works with our public office and can complete this task."

"Who runs this firm?" I asked.

"Me."

I couldn't even laugh. We were behind schedule and were pushing the Turks to catch up. Without an approved boiler we couldn't do lots of things. Like heat the building. This meant that not only could we not open for business, we'd have to keep using portable heaters inside so that we wouldn't ruin the finishes on the plaster and drywall. Summer ends quickly in St. Petersburg and we needed heat.

"So you're telling me that if I hired your private firm, you could get me the approved design I need."

"I can't guarantee it."

"Why not?" I asked.

"I can complete the design, but then it needs to be formally approved."

"By you?"

"Yes."

As a child I had seen a skit once on *The Carol Burnett Show*, in which a tourist tries to appeal his speeding ticket in a small Southern town where the cop, judge, and mayor are all the same person. But in the skit, those three people all work in unison. This schizophrenic official was trying to maintain the independence of each role.

"What if we don't redesign, or design *po-russki*, the boiler that is already built?" I asked.

"Then you have to have it tested, but you can't test it in my city. It's not safe, and once a boiler blew up and killed people. I have responsibility for the safety of the citizens of St. Petersburg and I won't allow you to do this."

How noble and inspiring this conversation was becoming. "The boiler is built into the fourth floor of our five-floor building," I said. "How can we test it outside of St. Petersburg?"

"You can cut a hole in the roof and get a helicopter to carry it to Finland, test it, and bring it back." He said this with authority and seemed convinced of its logic.

"Maybe it could work," Kleptov suggested.

Oh, my God, not now, I thought. This was worse than a bad TV comedy, and I knew Kleptov was already focusing on the deals he could make with the helicopter company. Absolutely insane.

"We cannot cut a hole in our roof," I said, "and we cannot decide this question today. We need to speak with our contractor to see what can be done about the testing and the design."

"Very well," the official said. "I will wait to hear from you."

Per the contract, our general contractor was responsible for securing all of the building permits required for the construction. We had fought like hell over this language, which called for one party to help as much as possible, but for the other party to ultimately be responsible for the result. Each party had eagerly tried to be the helper and promised the most diligent and far-reaching help possible, as long as the other party retained ultimate responsibility. We had won the fight and they were responsible, so we met with them and tried to work out an intelligent solution to the boiler problem that would not impede the project. Ultimately we did. The contractor was able to find a Russian designer, and the already built and installed boiler was *designed* and approved. Fire, aim, ready.

The run-up to the completion of any building is intense. Attempting to manage this one was just layered with more complexity. We had always tried to navigate between the normal way to manage a project and the requirement to gain all of the certifications and permits from the official public agencies. In the States, substantial completion can be agreed on between the contractor and the owner, and public officials don't really become involved until you need them to issue a certificate of occupancy.

When we negotiated our contract, I had figured Kemalco would not call for a formal Russian commission and a review by the local authorities until they were sure the building was ready. Otherwise they would risk too much interference from people they would normally want to keep at arm's length and see as little as possible. Since that was what I thought they would think, having the commission as part of our contractual milestone for substantial completion seemed like a great idea.

So they called for the commission and set a date. All of the subcontractors were invited, along with the fire commissioner and a few other officials. We gathered in the building at the appointed time. We walked slowly around and spent at most fifteen minutes looking at one of the retail spaces.

"Is everyone ready?" the contractor asked. When everyone said yes, he added, "Great. Let's go to lunch."

A complete fake out. The contractor had, according to tradition, arranged for a huge spread with lots of drinks at a nearby restaurant. Bottles were promptly opened and the commission began its working lunch.

"Aren't we going to look at the building?" I asked.

"We've seen it," they said.

During the lunch a *protokol* was prepared for each of the participants to sign. The contractor passed it around to each of his subs, who dutifully signed. They passed it to the fire inspector, who did not sign. He wanted to talk to me.

"Can you introduce me to each of your tenants?" he asked.

"They ... don't speak Russian very well," I said. "The other contractor works for the tenants and he is responsible for the building of each space. Is there a question you have?"

"I would like to meet them all," he said. "It's easier if I meet each one individually."

What a disaster, I thought. Not only had I totally missed the lack of any true significance to this commission, now I was supposed to be the shtetl matchmaker for our tenants to set up dates with the fire inspector. There wasn't the slightest chance I was going to play this role. "I need to be back at the office," I said. "It was nice to meet you."

I heard later that the lunch had gone on for some time. The commission *protokol* was ultimately signed, but not that day. In the meantime, we had our lender's representative work with our construction managers to draft the voluminous punch lists that would be part of our lives for the next several months.

Nigel, the lending supervisor, didn't like grand openings. "I always see people on stage whom I never saw during the whole building process. I skip grand openings whenever I can."

I was more enthusiastic. This was what we had waited for. Of course, our partners all saw the event from their own perspectives. For the Russians, and especially Kleptov, it was a social event in their city, and tickets were carefully guarded and doled out in the proper manner. We saw it as a marketing event, and we wanted every prospective tenant to show up and be feted with food, booze, and a VIP tour.

"Who are these people?" Kleptov asked when I handed him the list of the international firms from AmCham (American Chamber of Commerce) and SPIBA (St. Petersburg

International Business Association). "What do they have to do with our building?"

"They'll pay for it," I said, "if we can get them to sign leases. Have you noticed it's empty right now? We need to fill it up."

And, of course, in the run-up to the opening we needed to revisit all of the earlier battles I had thought were over. More legal bills, more compromises, more documents. To get the Russian partners to agree to pay the last $20,000 in lender legal bills, I had gotten our Western partners to agree to adding fanciful fish to the facade of the Atrium and a model of a sailing ship to the top of the fountain.

When one partner said he didn't like the ship, I said to him, "Please, this is not about a ship. We need peace in the kingdom."

The Atrium was beautiful as it neared the day of completion. We had turned the building inside out, with the most attractive facades on the inside of the glassed-in courtyard. The floor was magnificent with its detailed granite patterns, and the fountain added a nice peaceful sound and a central focal point. The glass peak of the actual atrium reflected sunlight into every corner. The dream of the building was coming into focus.

I remember walking out onto one of the balconies with Allan and telling him that the Atrium was a microcosm of Russia, a grand stage. I really did see Russia in that way, a grand stage where some of the greatest dramas of the twentieth century had been played out. A play where not all of the actors succeeded or survived. A lot of people had not passed the test of being there. Speaking of one Frenchman he had hired to be a bartender at their hotel restaurant, 300 Types of Russian Vodka, Mirsky once wistfully remarked, "He … ended badly."

None of us were good at everything we did. Richard P. and I had ordered the office furniture for our model office without asking for any advice. We were like newlywed husbands who decorated the living room without input from their wives. It had seemed like a good idea at the time. Allan, the architect, was furious when he saw how large the desks that we had ordered were and how they nearly filled the room. It was a minor glitch for me, and I loved sitting at the big desk. His point was well taken, though, that I should generally stay out of most discussions that had anything to do with aesthetics.

We blessed the building before it opened. I told my wife that we were planning to chase away all of the evil spirits. "How many priests did they bring?" she asked. Fair enough. But there is a nice photo of the two of us smiling at the end of the ceremony, standing in front of the running fountain. And I will long remember the toast I was able to give at the loud and raucous celebration dinner.

"In Chicago I was taught to think like a general," I started, alternating between English and Russian. "Mehmet approaches, we send in Tom. Tom gets into trouble, I call Chicago for air support. Allan, we need air support. Ralph, we need air support. When I really need help, I call Paul in London. Paul is an armored division. But here in Russia, the ground … moves. It doesn't stay where it was. Here you cannot think like a general. Here you must think like an admiral. So I'd like to propose a toast to our Chairman Academician

Mirsky and all of his naval support. Congratulations and thank you."

The crowd took a drink and gave me a nice round of applause. In that moment, only hours after I had been specifically uninvited to be part of a leadership photo in the atrium of the building, Ralph Walton came up to me on the stage and said directly in my ear, "They're clapping because *you* made this project happen, and everyone in this room knows that."

The next day, we all woke up hung over. Our Warsaw team and our Chicago team flew home, and we went back to work on the building. Kemalco had interrupted its crews' work for a three-day cleaning for the party, but we needed to actually finish the building, especially for BHS and the retail tenants on the first floor. We also desperately needed more office tenants to fill the other four floors. Since the US government and Urobank were our primary lenders, we had reserved their office space next to our model office on the third floor. Still, even the affiliates of our own lenders—Urobank and EXPOC—had yet to finalize their arrangements for leasing and building out their spaces. Unfinished business.

As Kemalco worked through the punch list, we continued to haggle over exactly how much of the completion delay was their fault. There was a $3,000 per day penalty for being late, and in the back of my head I was counting how many days it would take to match the $160,000 we had wasted at the start of construction. Ultimately we would agree to $120,000. Kemalco may have owed us more than that, but we simply extended their due date by enough days to match the agreed-upon amounts. Once the battle is over, there is no point to gloating. It makes a lot more sense to write the history in such a way that everyone can maintain his pride and move on in a positive manner. I bet a lot of history is written that way. Publicly we were all heroes after the grand opening, at least for a time.

CHAPTER 8

ESCAPE TO HYDRA

Both my wife and I needed a break from Russia longer than a Finnish weekend, so we planned a trip to Greece. We wanted to see the islands.

It turned out to be the first of many annual trips to Hydra. We had picked the place out of a borrowed paperback guidebook because the description said there were no cars on the island and it was only about an hour and a half by hydrofoil from Athens. Our one-year-old son Charlie was just starting to walk, and we didn't want him to be run over by one of the many minibikes or motorcycles that are popular on these islands. Over the next four years, we returned every May to stay at a former sponge factory that was now a lovely, small hotel. On that first trip in May 1998, we had reservations in a more rustic "resort" on the edge of the island.

We approached the dock as the hydrofoil began to settle down back into the water. These boats looked exactly like primitive spacecraft from 1950s black and white sci-fi movies, with a glass bubble cockpit and round windows in a single line along the white hull. They used the same boats in St. Petersburg to ferry tourists across the Gulf of Finland to Peter the Great's Summer Palace. The bow of the hydrofoil would rise up to a fifteen-degree angle as the craft reached full speed and then settle back into the water as it approached the dock. This was our third stop from Athens on that trip. In Greece the hydrofoils served as a kind of funky long-distance water taxi. As we settled down into the low waves and chugged toward the stone wall of the dock, my wife and I were finally starting to relax.

We were on this vacation with my parents and had just spent two days in Athens. Visiting the Acropolis, a dream of mine for many years, was now fulfilled. We saw it first at night from the balcony of our hotel rooms, and then hiked up and all over its grounds the following day. Wonderful.

Athens itself was not relaxing. I was so wound up from dealing with all the bureaucrats in Russia, I couldn't slow down. "They are as many as sands upon the beach," I told one traveling acquaintance I met in the airport, then felt like a deranged person after I said it. He and the other travelers around me shifted uneasily, their radar alerted. I was so wound up, I had a hard time with stupid little things.

"Is the breakfast included?" I asked the waiter at our hotel in Athens.

"Yes," he answered.

"Good, we'll take a table for four."

"Here is your bill," the manager told us at the end of the meal.

"No. I asked and was told it was included."

"Yes, but the person who said that was incompetent."

No shit. More crap to argue about. And knowing the play on words made it worse. It was the same translation the Russians would use. *Nikompetentni* doesn't mean incompetent the way Americans use the word, as in idiot. It means "does not have the authority" to make such a decision. So the hotel manager was technically correct. The waiter didn't have the authority to tell us the breakfast was included, but the incident came across like the typical fleecing of the guests. In Bulgaria they used to offer you fruit for dessert and then charge you for each piece separately, as if you had ordered five servings, so that your dessert bill was higher than the entrée. I thought this misunderstanding over breakfast was a similar move, and I was too wound up to just smile and let it go. It's sort of funny now, but it wasn't then.

So here we were approaching the dock. The Greek crew moves quickly. They unload our collection of small and medium suitcases and a few bags. They are really nice to Charlie and any other toddler. They seem to love all kids. We have arrived.

The dock is paved with large cobblestones. We are deposited in the midst of a bustling and beautiful tourist port. Every square foot that isn't a loading area is an outdoor café. The small, brightly colored sailboats and fishing boats tied up in the harbor look they belong in a Monet painting. It's warm and sunny and we are on break. No hurry at all.

And then they descend. Probably not meaning to be as pushy as they were, but they descend. The donkey drivers, three or four of them, in my face.

"Take the donkey" "Need a ride?" "Give us the bags!" "Here, I'll help."

"No." I lose it. "No! Leave us alone! We just got here. We don't know where we are going. We are not in a hurry to get there. Go away!"

My mother looks concerned. She hasn't ever seen me act like this.

I settle down. We sit down at a café and I have a large Heineken. I walk back to the donkey drivers.

"Sorry," I say, and tell them which of the small hotels we're going to.

"No problem. Very close."

"How much?"

"Five people? These bags?"

We easily agree on a price, hop up on three donkeys, and they slowly trot us down the narrow cobblestone road—the only real road on the island—around the bend, and maybe just under a mile to our hotel. The resort is actually a collection of small cabanas and one restaurant on a stony beach. The guidebook had said it was the only beach on the island, so we picked it, but we're not real beach people.

My mother hates the sun. She had just moved to Arizona with my father, but that's another story.

We take some cute photos of my parents and my son at the beach, but we don't last long at the resort. I think we stayed only one night. One look at the tiny latches that supposedly locked the door at night—more like you'd use on a kitchen cabinet—and my parents are not comfortable. "It's not secure," my dad says conclusively. *From what?* I think. There can't be more than a few hundred people staying on the island on any given day. It's a resort for tourists. They aren't going to rob us. And we're at the end of the donkey road. There aren't more than a dozen people here. Doesn't matter. We need to find a new place to stay.

We go back to the port, this time by a small power boat with an outboard engine. It's like a big rowboat with a little sun canopy over the top. The wind kicks up and we get sprayed with water. The boat heaves up and down. We sit our son in the backpack and set it in the bottom of the boat so he is more secure. It's May and not that warm if you're not sitting in the sun. Getting sprayed with sea water in the shade of the canopy, we are slightly chilled.

We wander the town on foot. I like to walk and it's an interesting little town. We find one cute hotel. I think it's fine, but my parents want to keep looking. We wind our way through the alley-like streets, and I hope I can remember where to find the hotel we just rejected in case we don't find another one.

It makes me laugh, the differences between the way we travel, my parents and I. My father pays as little as possible for a cheap flight, endures the discomfort, takes a jitney cab in London, thereby adding a few hours to the ride from the airport, but then wants to stay at the five-star Grosvenor House Hotel. I use frequent flyer miles when I have them to fly business class, but then find hotels that are modest and well located. And my father is hardly skittish. Once, after I explained that my father had been a lawyer for the government, Slova asked me, "So what would he do if you got into trouble here, call the FBI?"

"No, he's not like that," I answered. "He'd call the air force."

Eventually we stumble across the Bratsera, through a small doorway gate and into its courtyard. A pure white canvas canopy stretches over the restaurant on the left. In the center of the courtyard is a pool. Otherwise you would have to swim in the Aegean off the rocks. Surrounding the pool are small adobe-style buildings with individual rooms, all entered from the courtyard. And on the ground are the snails that Charlie loves, which eat the basil growing in the shade of the trellises. The old sponge factory building itself has been redesigned as a large meeting area to accommodate a small conference.

The hotel is hardly modern. For several years, we have to fax our reservations with the credit-card information filled in by hand on their form. Now anyone can do it on their website. But even in the web images, it still looks beautiful, peaceful, and quaint.

The wood of the structures was hewn, old, and rich looking. With the tables next to the pool, we could eat dinner and drink wine while the baby—then later a boy—slept in the room nearby. We could see the door of the room across the pool. No need for a sitter. Just beautiful.

For lunch or dinner we pick out tiny restaurants with different views. My parents buy a painting of one of these views; it still hangs in their entry hall in Virginia. On later trips we learn that the alley next to our table that is shown in the painting leads to the small beach where young men carry the cross down into the water and then back out as part of their Easter celebration, a kind of resurrection play. Easter is a very big deal in the Orthodox world. Purification. Resurrection.

The island is like that. All the Greek islands are like that. An escape. Timeless. Not for everyone, though. My father has had enough after a day or so and starts talking about finding a golf course. When we suggest sitting at one of the harbor cafés, he responds that we've already done that. He has a harder time going along with the idea of doing nothing. Just not his personality.

A few years earlier, when we worked in Bulgaria, my wife and I used to drive five hours to Thásos. As soon as the ferry left the mainland, we had the feeling that all of the nonsense was staying behind on the dock. Just loading the ferry boat was a trip all its own. Young guys directed the drivers as if we were in some kind of evacuation. They were impatient with nervous tourists like me, who didn't want to scratch the company's Ford Escort we had borrowed for the weekend. One time a young Greek guy shook his head and escorted me out of the driver's seat. He got in and quickly swung the car into the tiny irregular space that was so clear in his mind and so improbable in mine.

Not a bad metaphor for a lot of these encounters. Each person not against the other, just not getting at all what the other is seeing or how it could work. More frustrated than angry at first, in part at the inability to communicate precisely. And then angry in part because of the sense that, "If you just would let me do it, you would see the good result, move on and be happy. Relax."

Timeless. Not in the sense of ancient, but more in the sense of the eternity of the moment, an idea I first learned from a book by Gabriel García Márquez. Not worrying about time, not interested in time. A true escape from a manic sense of scheduling.

Even a two-day weekend escape feels like such a release, you don't mind starting it up again the following week.

I love it. I love the taste of honey in the yogurt while having breakfast next to the pool. I am always up earlier than my wife, and Charlie and I would go eat while she stayed in bed. Then Charlie would go look for snails. Or talk to the waiters. Or play with the pretty blonde Russian girl who is also staying there.

On our first visit, my wife and I take Charlie in his baby backpack on a hike up to the top of the mountain, where there is a monastery. We start on the road and climb quickly as it becomes a path. What I remember most is the air. As we climb we pass through the pine trees, and the breeze makes such an incredible scent of fresh pine air. It is warm in the sun but not too hot, and the cool air is perfectly refreshing. And so quiet. You can hear the breeze swishing through the pine branches or pushing the tall grass back and forth.

It takes some time to get to the top. I don't remember how much time, but we didn't bother to bring any lunch, just some water. From the top of the hills we can see how small the port is and how dry the rest of the island is. The harbor looks small enough from the dock; from the top of the hill it looks absolutely tiny. The island was only settled in the 1700s. There is no water other than what is collected from roofs into cisterns and whatever supply is carried by the old midsized freighter that shuttles back and forth, bringing water for the current residents.

We look for pirate flags with our son, something we do in any harbor, even along Chicago's lakefront. Charlie loves pirates and thinks they are quite real. Once we flew to Finland when he was older to take him to the North Pole. Lisa walked him around the corner of a wooden lodge early one morning, and they suddenly stumbled upon Santa Claus, sitting all alone at his desk and working on his list with a huge quill pen. Charlie froze in his tracks and then quickly sat down on a bench next to his mother. A Russian boy walked past and Santa spoke to him in Russian. Then Santa asked Charlie in English where he is from. "Warsaw," Charlie said. "Oh, *djien dobry*, Charlie," Santa said, of course speaking instantly in Polish. I will never forget that. No boundary at all between the real world and the world of enchanted fantasy.

The sight of one large yacht in the harbor at Hydra makes me smile. Metaxa has invited their best high-rolling customers on a cruise. I don't have to listen right next to the boat to guess correctly that the party ship is filled with Russians.

Our first Hydra vacation is ending. We leave the island a day early so we can be at a hotel near the Athens airport in preparation for our early-morning plane trip back to Russia. That hotel is a nightmare, filled with loud teenagers celebrating their first beers and drinking in the hallways while we try to put our baby son to sleep. And the rooftop bar next to the runway is hardly as quiet and peaceful as tiny tables set along cobblestone streets. But at least my father has found a golf course.

On the short ride to the airport, we have one last run-in with the taxi drivers in Athens, who invent charges and pay scales and twice use a kind of flimflam with local currency to basically give us change for ten dollars after we've given them the equivalent of a hundred dollars. This is in the days of the drachma, before the euro. The cab drivers are a special breed. I pay the last one what I think we owe him and tell him we simply aren't going to pay the other fees because we have been ripped off one too many times.

"Fuck you," are the last words from his mouth as we walk away toward the door of the airport terminal.

I forgive him and all their sins. I love being there and have always loved going back to Greece. I hope I always do.

CHAPTER 9

SUMMER CRISES 1998

"What does Mirsky want?" I asked.
"Mirsky wants more tenants," Slova answered.
"I can't let you bet the company," Paul Barron said.

Back in the winter of 1997, Paul Barron wasn't buying our proposal to resolve a sticking point with our anchor retail tenant, Britansky Dom, the Russian franchisee for British Home Stores (BHS). BHS wanted us, as landlord, to guarantee the amount of time it would take to register their lease with the local tax authorities. BHS couldn't open for business until they were registered for sales tax, and to register for sales tax they needed to register their lease at the property. Hassan Bagai, the franchisee, was in his thirties and from a wealthy Middle-Eastern family. He was comfortable with gambling and had proposed that we pay a daily late fee after a certain date. He was quick to make deals and was eager to keep moving. Our team in St. Petersburg was also eager to sign a deal with an anchor tenant that would take virtually the whole first floor of our building. Hassan's senior advisor, Neel Mahatra, was his guiding hand, and he thought the deal could work. But there was no way Barron was going to gamble on a deadline for yet another Russian permit.

Barron and the rest of our board had bought into my pitch of BHS as our "credit" tenant, a more pedestrian but safer alternative than the high-brow Cartier licensee. Cartier wanted one small shop—not an entire floor—but it did offer the hope of attracting a luxurious mix of small boutiques, more in tune with our Class A building. The young, short, bearded, and slightly effeminate licensee had come to our apartment office wearing a half-dozen Cartier and other gold accessories; and with his own bodyguard, who sat silently, earpiece and all, and stared at the door the whole time. On his second visit to our office, the licensee's face was partially bandaged and stitched up. I naturally, if rudely, stared.

"It was an accident," he said. "A bomb went off in my hallway, but it was meant for my neighbor."

I guessed the licensee was about my age. I didn't have a bodyguard. I didn't know anyone who got blown up accidentally outside his own apartment. I looked again at the bodyguard. I imagined trying to collect past-due rent from him. A licensee isn't even a franchisee. The name *Cartier* describes only the right of the store to sell a certain brand of merchandise, and doesn't entail any financial support from the French parent company. The board didn't have to live in Russia, but I did.

"Please," I said to the board, "let's drop Cartier and go with BHS."

Our British partners hesitated. For Americans, BHS was a foreign brand. To them, it was like a Woolworth's five-and-dime.

Barron sometimes spoke with a British accent—he talked about our *shedule*, not *schedule*—but he was pure Big Apple New York. We went with BHS. Ultimately, we agreed on a modified deal that we couldn't collect their security deposit—about half a million dollars—until we, as landlord, had fully registered their lease. This made both sides comfortable. Our board told us to make sure we got it done.

So we did. In October 1997, Viki, our supposed HR manager, achieved her finest moment. Viki occupied whatever position we needed to identify for her. She started out tidying up the office and eventually became head of human resources for the new building. I was fine with this. Walton owned 9 percent of the company and our Russian partner owned 40 percent. I didn't micromanage the payroll.

"Get some boxes of chocolate, nice ones, and meet me tomorrow," Viki told me. "We'll need the whole day."

The lease registration paperwork had to move from one small office to another. In typical fashion, each office maintained its own glacial schedule for moving paper back and forth. On Tuesdays, papers would go from office A to office B. Papers would not be sent back until the following week, or something like that. Viki had worked in this system for years. She knew the people and had the right temperament to handle them. All we did was play Federal Express Ground for a day. At 10 a.m. she and I drove up to the alley outside the first office. Viki took the application papers, one of the boxes of chocolates, and told me to wait. An hour later she was back, and we went searching for the next office and the next chocolate deposit. By midafternoon we were back at the first office, having shaved maybe two to three weeks off the process.

How could I explain to the office in Chicago why I was playing chauffer, sitting in an alley outside some rundown, dingy apartment-office building? "Is this what we pay you for?" they'd ask, but I knew they really only wanted to hear about results. "Is the lease registered yet?" was the question.

"Give me two weeks," I told Chicago. "Don't ask me to repeat what someone just told me about the process, because if I do then you'll think I'm crazy and I've been here too long. When it's done, I'll tell you. And then later, over a drink on your next visit to Russia, I'll explain how it happened. For now just give me two weeks. I think we'll get it done."

I had read the Foreign Corrupt Practices Act several times before coming to work in Russia. There was nothing in it about chocolate.

We got the lease registered, but then I moved on to other things before coming back to collecting the security deposit. The security deposit would come in the form of a letter of credit. That meant agreeing with the issuing bank and the lenders on how to formulate the actual documents. More discussions. Would our lenders accept the tenant's bank as creditworthy? If another bank were needed, would a bank acceptable to our lenders actually provide the letter of credit to a recently formed special-purpose company? And could we ever cash the letter of credit if we needed to? In the meantime, we needed more tenants; and the tenants we had already signed leases with needed their interior spaces built.

So I put the $500,000 letter of credit aside, ignoring a personal rule to always focus on the biggest money item first. We had a smaller retail tenant, Alphagraphics, that used the same bank in Moscow as BHS. I figured we could work out a document acceptable to our lenders for the smaller deposit, and then I'd use the same document to get the BHS deposit in place. The security deposit was just a backup anyway. The cash flow for our company during the final construction and initial leasing period was still based primarily on remaining disbursements from our EXPOC and Urobank loans.

I had had my nice vacation break to Hydra in May 1998, but now as June approached, I was trying to catch up with the constantly moving project. I wanted to finish things in order. First construction, then leasing, then property management. That is the rolling logic of development, but the whole process is like a fabric. All of these issues are woven together and the loose ends create constant distractions. Although publicly the construction of the main core building under the Kemalco contract was completed, we still had many issues to resolve with the handover. Since my childhood in suburban New Jersey, I had had an urge to bring order to a place, especially with construction. My brother would build something like a deck, and I'd clean up the pieces and finish painting it. I hated seeing things left undone. I could muster a lot of perseverance, and that had helped me gather accomplishments, like becoming an Eagle Scout, earning high honors at Exeter or developing a medical center in Chicago. But Russia was not Chicago, and tidying up after the last act meant less focus on the next scene and the new wave of actors coming onto the stage.

We had made peace with Kemalco in March 1998, signing an extension of the completion date that effectively reduced their delay penalty to an acceptable level for all parties. And the document didn't assign blame or point fingers. It was simply a contractual change order. All parties saved face. We got back the money I had paid in the beginning of the project for the early-start "management fees," and Kemalco got some recognition that they didn't create all of the various reasons why the completion date had been moved back. Plus, this was a private document. Publicly we had all praised Kemalco for their completion of the building at the grand opening back in November 1997. It is always easier to write a complete summary ex post facto that could never be written at the time, because parts of it would be simply untrue.

With the base building finally resolved, we were free to focus on the interior improvements to make each individual space ready for actual occupancy. I tried to hand off that work as much as possible to our Walton construction team, led by Tom Hands. Harry Marin had started to wind down his involvement in the project, and that allowed Tom to take a more active role without always looking over his shoulder.

I loved working with Tom. He was maybe a little over caffeinated, but his heart was in the right place and most of the tenants had nothing but positive things to say about him. Problem solver, energetic, committed. Tom couldn't speak a word of Russian, but that wasn't his job. I told Tom, "Your job is to tell me clearly whether the building will stand up straight, not to interpret the crazy rules. I'll deal with the Russians." If he got caught up offering crazy compromises to navigate all the rules, then I would have lost focus on whether what was he was telling me was actually true, or just something that he thought could be an acceptable solution.

Tom once lost his temper with our Russian architect, Soska, a respected senior figure who had served as historic conservator for the city and had, after all, successfully negotiated for our new Krasotsky entrance. But the architect was not being responsive on some matter. At a weekly construction meeting, he was supposed to bring some designs, but instead brought a letter explaining why he wasn't ready. With the architect's son and assistant sitting next to him at the table, Tom took the letter, tore it into pieces, and threw it up in the air like confetti.

"You have a hard job, Tom," I told him later, "because you need to first go and apologize to the architect, and then you need to get back on his case so he finishes those plans."

Tom got along well with the expat tenants because they all understood that he was fighting to make them happy and get their spaces open as soon as possible. He was creative as an architect as well. We created a mezzanine floor for the private office of the Norwegian ambassador, both to save space and to take advantage of skylight windows that were otherwise too high up to let anyone using the space enjoy the incredible views. Tom came up with solutions on how to increase the heating and ventilation capacity for a classroom in the Japanese consulate, designed for larger crowds than our original design would have supported; and he even bumped out some of the interior atrium walls a few feet in order to add more leasable area. He made a lot of contributions to the building. Later he and I would be the only Walton staff to earn bonuses in a year when the US economy performed poorly.

Tom's job was made easier by our unbelievably reliable and somehow low-key Russian interior contractor, Pace. Two young partners ran this firm, and they quietly did exactly what they said they were going to do. They were learning as they went—installing drywall, dropped ceilings, lighting, and variable air volume (VAV) systems for a Class A office building in a world that had no experience with such things. They were open, honest, flexible, and trustworthy. They didn't share everything with me, and I wasn't interested as long as we were meeting our schedule.

"You know," one of them once told me, "not everything can be on the books, but all firms must work in this way to some extent."

I trusted them. They helped our project succeed, and we helped their company grow.

There were few such people. We needed more. Or maybe I needed to hand off more of the responsibilities and should have stopped trying to play and replay the entire game of the project in my mind. My head was starting to explode from the pressure. New issues were leaking out, escaping my sense of control. I was so glad about the settlement on construction and the steady progress with leasing. These were wins, and they were well received as wins by the board and our company in Chicago. Urobank and Walton were clearly more focused on Warsaw now. In retrospect, those wins on construction were like Pyrrhic victories. They cost so much of my time, I left management issues unaddressed.

Nikolai, our property manager, had Western real-estate experience from working for a Western brokerage and development firm that had come to Russia early, just after the collapse of Communism, and he had had some success. Bright and with a dry sense of humor, he was older than me and smoked cigarettes like many Russians. Since I liked to run, I teased him about his health. "If you don't smoke," he told me, "you will die healthy." While he was professional and diligent in his approach to real-estate and company matters, Nikolai was ill-suited personality-wise to engage with Kleptov. Kleptov knew he had many more connections and bureaucratic savvy than Nikolai, and probably wondered why we even needed a professional property manager for Walton when Kleptov was already the assistant director. This situation left Nikolai doing the grunt work of actually running the building while Kleptov was free to pursue his robust appetite for distractions.

Nor was I experienced in property management at a corporate level. I had managed a 16,000-square-foot medical building in Chicago after we developed it, but that was five times smaller and all office, not mixed use, and not in Russia. Walton had a good team of property managers in Warsaw led by the *przezsh* (president) of our local Polish affiliate, but so far his presence in St. Petersburg had been limited to a one-day on-the-job seminar, much of which was taken up with arranging his personal dry cleaning and hygiene at the Grand Hotel Europe. He had flown in on an early-morning flight from Warsaw only two hours away, but somehow he was not available to meet us until two in the afternoon.

For me, it was frustrating having to manage the building since our number of company employees went way up, from seven to fifty. I couldn't ignore the Russian staff as I had more or less during the development.

"The guards are hungry," Viki, our HR manager, had yelled at me during the frenetic days leading to our grand opening, "because you haven't given the order for them to eat!"

I didn't even know how to respond to such a ridiculous remark. The guards were all healthy, strong former naval officers in their twenties and thirties. All had been recommended by Mirsky's group, and I had let our main partner manage them. The idea that I should I have to tell them to eat seemed as stupid as telling them to breathe. I should have allowed a bit of translation leeway. Perhaps she meant I hadn't set up their free lunches with a local restaurant. The paternal/maternal society so ingrained in them remained so totally foreign to me, despite my pretensions that I had gotten used to being in Russia.

On the other hand, I loved our new office, loved finally being inside the building we had worked so hard to create. I could stand at my desk on our third floor and look out into the atrium, see all the colors change, see the sky, and see all of the visitors who came into the building—who they were and who they were going to see. I loved being there, finally out of the shitty apartment. My office had interior window walls as well, so I could always see my staff. I set up my desk deliberately facing Nikolai's in our shared room so he could see and hear every conversation I had; learning in this way so he could ultimately assume the role of property manager. We also could both easily see the ongoing progress of other tenants on the third floor—Urobank, the US consulate—as well as the fourth floor, where the Japanese consulate and Norwegian consulate were considering space.

The beautiful atrium wasn't the whole story. We had signed some leases, but we were not doing so well collecting the rent. Only five months after opening, BHS was already falling behind. So was Special Health Care, our sole office tenant at the time of the grand opening. Even Urobank, our main partner and original funder, was declaring that they would not pay their rent for technical reasons. The crescendo was starting to build by June 1998, when I returned from my vacation to Greece and picked up the issues of the security deposits and letters of credit. To cap it off, we needed yet another Moscow Central Bank permit, this time for the opening of a debt service reserve account. Why not? Why should any issue ever be fully settled?

The best way to get to Moscow was to take an early one-way flight. I could depart St. Petersburg at around seven a.m., arrive by nine, and take a cab to the center of Moscow for a first meeting at eleven. Even in 1998, the traffic in Moscow was horrible and businesses were spread out across different parts of the city. I never found it possible to schedule more than three meetings in a day there, since it typically took up to an hour to travel between offices. To get that third meeting, I needed to schedule it late in the afternoon. The meeting could stretch into dinner and drinks, so I'd avoid the evening rush-hour traffic back to the airport. Instead, I'd wait until ten or eleven p.m. and catch a taxi to Kievsky Vogzal for a sleeper train back to St. Petersburg, which left at midnight. By eight the next morning, I would be back in my apartment in St. Petersburg, taking a shower and getting ready for work.

So I went to Moscow on July 6. I anticipated closing the deal with Alphagraphics on the basement space in the building. By coincidence, Alphagraphics used the same bank, Dogovor Bank, as BHS. The good news was that we were signing Alphagraphics, but Dogovor had started to intimate that there were problems with BHS. I finally asked if the bank would issue us the letter of credit.

"No, we will not," they said. "You need to meet with BHS."

I was getting the sense that I was late checking on the barn door.

BHS had told us that they were having problems. We were not collecting our rent, initially for "technical reasons." Information trickled out that their sales were less than expected. Kitayski Dom (Chinese House) was the local nickname for the Britansky Dom store, because many of the goods were made in China, not Great Britain.

"Don't worry," BHS told me. "We will pay you the rent, just in installments. We are trying to liquidate some of our stock and create cash for new merchandise. We realize our initial merchandise and price points were not what the market wanted. So we need to dump these goods at a discount and then build up cash flow to pay for new goods. By the fall we hope to be in much better shape. However, on the letter of credit, we are not sure how to make you happy. Your bank, Urobank, wouldn't accept a letter of credit from our initial bank, and now with our drop in cash flow, even that bank is shy about extending the letter of credit to us."

From my limited two-year banking experience at Shorebank, I understood that BHS was in a classic fast-growth cash flow scenario for any small business. They were illiquid, and they had made a strategic error by investing earlier surplus cash into the bricks and mortar of their Moscow store. That would save them rental expenses years in the future, but right now they needed cash flow for operations. The down payment on the building in Moscow was of no use in achieving this.

Meanwhile our initial office tenant, Special Health Care, was experiencing its own problems and also not paying its rent. SHC had been positioned for us as a small Czech company affiliated with a large hospital. It was an early form of medical tourism. Their office had an enormous television set and couch in the waiting room, with a small bowl of Ferrero Rocher chocolates on a table in front of the couch. The purpose of the office was to show wide-screen videos of the procedures available at the Czech hospital. SHC would then make travel arrangements for Russians to use the facilities. It wasn't proceeding very successfully though, because wealthy Russians who would consider traveling to the "West" for medical procedures wanted to fly to southern France, not the Czech Republic, a former Communist bloc state.

As I started conversations with Dusbek, the head of their local office, I realized the unpeeling of the onion was becoming so ridiculous, I couldn't make any of it up. First, the "special" procedure they were promoting on their wide-screen TV was penile enlargement.

"This is an established medical specialty!" Dusbek said when I shook my head, unable to suppress a giggle.

It got even worse. After that I met with Dusbek's boss, who was angry because he suspected that the reason sales were slow at the St. Petersburg office was because Dusbek was focusing all of his time on his other personal venture, a dog-food import business. So penile enlargement and dog-food imports. Our first Class A tenant. Why not?

In the course of the negotiations for SHC's lease, Dusbek had signed a letter of credit that was contingent on him acknowledging the invoice. Since we had the signed invoice, I thought we could simply collect on the letter of credit and be done with discussions about dog food. Not so fast. My initial attempt to cash the Czech letter of credit in Russia did not go well.

"You need a permit to do this and you don't have it," our Franco-German-Russian banker told me.

"What if I just cash it?" I asked. "What's the penalty?"

"One hundred percent fine plus fees."

So if I cashed in the $30,000 letter of credit, I would lose more than $30,000. Sure, why not? The clear image in my head was of pulling the trigger on a gun and watching the gun explode in my hand. Obviously, this wasn't going to work. I needed to switch gears and focus on something else until I could figure this out.

Urobank was also behind in its rent. There was a nuance to the VAT (value added tax) laws that required Urobank to pay VAT and then get it back later. Accountants in the London head office had determined that, as an international organization, Urobank did not have to pay VAT period, and they were refusing to pay the rent on principle. They suggested paying the rent without VAT. Maya, our Russian accountant, told me this would have to be counted as a smaller rent payment that included VAT, since we had our own VAT forms to file. VAT is a kind of universal policing, where each business is both a collector and a payer. Everyone is a policeman. It seems genetically programmed into Europeans of all kinds and is completely antithetical to US business's way of thinking.

This became a bullfight between Urobank and us. I knew if we accepted the smaller payment, we would never get the VAT. However, I also knew that if we ever reported to the Russian partners on our board that Urobank, as a tenant, had not paid its rent, it would create enough of a scandal that they would be forced to pay the whole amount. Plus, it seemed to me from the information I had that Maya was correct—she almost always was—and that Urobank's head office knew this as well, but they didn't want to back down or go through the local process of getting their registration done. They were so used to telling everyone else the importance of playing by the rules in the brave new world we were creating, they neglected to see the significance of their own example. So on the issue of the Urobank rent I stood there, cape in hand, and figured that although the suspense was going to increase, we would, like the bullfighter, ultimately win. It would just take a little courage.

Our cash flow at that point in the project was dependent on the continuing disbursements of our proceeds from the

Urobank and EXPOC loans, much more so than from the initial rents. Our first interest payments were due to these lenders, and they would need to be paid from the next disbursement, scheduled for early July. The disbursement application was submitted in June. If we missed the interest payments, we would be in default. We were actually at the edge of a default, and we might or might not have entered a period where an event, with the passage of time, led to a default. Had we crossed the line? Maybe, maybe not. I was determined to get the disbursement, make the interest payments, and then declare the default event. Otherwise, I feared a chain reaction of defaults that we would not be able to recover from. It was like a demonstration I had seen once of a room filled with Ping-Pong balls set on mousetraps. Once the first one went off, the whole room quickly became a shooting gallery.

The disbursements were made July 7. We sent the default notification on July 14 that BHS had not paid its rent nor delivered its security deposit. Urobank's new board member, Diana, was beyond furious at what she felt was a clear deception and violation of their trust in us as the developer. She demanded a board meeting immediately. As I sat in the office one night in St. Petersburg, the battle began with a barrage of faxes. Everyone else had gone home. I was at my desk looking out the window at the lovely, lit atrium when it began to hit my nerves.

Beep, beep. The first fax from Urobank arrived, a letter explaining what they understood had happened. *Beep, beep.* A declaration of loan default. *Beep, beep.* The agenda for the board meeting with a long list of items. The final one: Item G.

"Determination of the disposition of the General Director." A firing squad.

I felt very much alone the next day. I told the staff that the next few weeks were going to be difficult, but that we would need to get through it. *We.* I could sense from the lack of direct looks at me that staff members were already planning for their own futures more than mine. But the reaction from our head office in Chicago was one of total support.

Just as Diana was the thirtyish replacement at Urobank in London for the more seasoned Paul Barron, Roger Glass had recently been promoted to take over the Walton role held by Allan James. Paul and Allan had actually left at the same time in order to form a real-estate fund together. Roger was totally in my corner. He began by buying time.

"We can't meet right away because of some other priorities in Chicago," Roger told Diana. "Ralph Walton's schedule won't permit it. Let's plan for an August meeting instead of July."

"But I'll be on leave in August," Diana protested.

"Oh. I didn't know that," Roger replied. "Could someone else attend instead?"

Roger was punting to gain field position. Meanwhile, Ralph called Diana and spoke to her more directly. "Do you realize," he asked, "that I have one million dollars of my *own* money in this project? How much of your *own* personal money do you have invested in this project? Please don't tell me that we are not committed to this project. Let us send some of our senior people to St. Petersburg so we can get to the bottom of the situation. We promise to keep you fully informed."

Richard Sloan was more circumspect but also supportive. "We don't have a security deposit right now," he told Diana. "If we fire Glenn, we won't have a general director either, and we still won't have a security deposit. We should think about this. Who would replace him?"

In the meantime, Maya informed me that Urobank would pay their rent in full with the VAT. We also heard indirectly that Diana had been perplexed when our interest payment arrived at Urobank. Reacting to the duplicity of the disbursement approval, she had expected nothing but the worst. Maybe when she saw that the interest payments were being made as required, she hesitated and allowed for more time to fully understand what was going on.

So the date of the Krasotsky 23 board meeting was moved to July 30, and the Walton team came to St. Petersburg in mid-July. I had my doubts about everything at that point, but the Walton team—and Ralph especially—kept repeating to me, "You have our full support. We are in your corner." I heard it many times, but I was slow to let down my guard and fully accept it. Right up until the board meeting itself, I told our attorney in Washington, DC, that I wasn't sure how to prepare for the board meeting. Should I bring an armful of binders to address any questions that could be raised? Or should I bring one small, thin envelope with a letter that would not take long to translate? The letter would be formal and polite, thanking all for the opportunity to have served for the past three years, but the simultaneous verbal message I wanted to offer would be something more crude and direct like, "After all I have done, you can each one of you please f—— yourselves."

I had been overseas for five years by the summer of 1998. My wife and I had never sold our three-story condo apartment built into a former church on the southwest side of Chicago, with its fireplace, deck, hot tub, and manageable $1,500 per month mortgage. Every time we flew back to Europe from Chicago, I automatically stored the tickets for the next return flight in my nightstand next to the bed. I put every ounce of my energy into these projects, but since we never knew how things would work out, we were always prepared to simply go home. In 2002, we would do just that and fly home from Poland, but it could easily have been from Russia in 1998.

Before I made any decisions that summer, I needed to understand how the Russian partners would react. They owned 50 percent of the company; and no matter what Urobank wanted to do, if Neptune and the city didn't support the Urobank action, then nothing would happen. Long believers in democratic centralism, the two Russian partners always voted together. And the Russian partners couldn't figure out what I had done to make Diana so mad. They were not as focused on the nuances of the disbursement requests and the default provisions in the loan agreement. It was my job to manage those documents, and they didn't value the small details as much as the big picture. I gradually heard back that they understood that, in essence, what I had done was take some liberties with the documents for the purposes of securing more actual dollars from our lender for our project. They decided I wasn't doing it for myself as much as for the project.

"For this we close our eyes," one later told me.

To me, it had to be that way—the project, our company, and then me. The alternative approach was me first, then my company, then the project. That approach was clearly visible in my codirector and all around me in Russia. It was an attitude that typically and predictably resulted in no project. I had to act first as general director for the Atrium, then as development director for Walton. Two weeks before the board meeting, I met with Alex Slova privately and asked him point blank whether Mirsky was going to send me home. His response was brief and clear. "What does Mirsky want?" he repeated. "Mirsky wants more tenants."

My relief was instantaneous and enormous. That was 59 percent of the votes on the board. We would win. It was a pivotal moment, when I realized that the US group hired by Urobank to keep an eye on the Russians had just enlisted the Russians on our side. The power of a hinge—it swings either way and plays a critical role connecting the two sides. For some reason neither of the two main partners could talk to each other directly, but only through us. I truly felt like a matador. The situation was still dangerous, but now clearly moving in my favor. Olé.

We got to work. We started collecting bits and pieces of money from BHS and the other tenants. "Mr. Workout!" Glass would exclaim over the phone at each piece of money or information I was able to secure. The Walton team scoured the lease agreements and assisted our local property manager to make sure we had all of the required insurance policies, etc. And our leasing efforts began to bear fruit.

First, I gave up on the letter of credit from Dusbek, and instead sent our own attack fax on July 17. I dropped the letter in like a mortar round, and then Kleptov and I arrived at their office together just minutes after our declaration of their default. I got the idea from the movie *Platoon*, where each Viet Cong soldier carried one mortar rocket. After loading his rocket in the mortar, he ran forward. Our leases stated clearly that after a default, anything left in the premises would belong to the landlord. There was no timeframe stated for how much time after the default. So five minutes seemed like enough time for a country with an emerging legal system.

When Kleptov and I arrived at their office on that Friday, we told SHC they had three days to get all of their furniture out of the office. Otherwise we would seize everything as partial payment for their back rent. I thought it was a great idea because we had an appointment to show the space to Deutsche Bank on the following Tuesday. DB needed a rapid move-in date and would not be interested in a space encumbered by legal claims. The Russian partners praised me for my focus on the big picture, but they berated Kleptov at the same time.

"We understand how Glenn thinks as an American, but you are a Russian. You should have gotten the TV set. That was a nice TV."

Deutsche Bank! A Class A tenant for a Class A building. Deutsche Bank verses Dusbek? The hell with the TV set. When the board meeting convened July 30, Mirsky began by asking if there was any news on the progress of filling the building. I told him yes and slid three leases across the table, asking for board approval to execute leases with Deutsche Bank, the Norwegian consulate, and the Japanese consulate.

"Oh, very nice," he said.

More tenants, I thought. and pretty fast too. Less than two weeks for Deutsche Bank. Not bad.

The meeting ran smoothly and went by fast. Urobank had sent one of their construction-oversight staff from London, whom none of us in St. Petersburg knew very well. He sat silently for almost the entire meeting. Mirsky had summarized the progress on the building and started to wish everyone a pleasant weekend, when the Urobank representative interrupted.

"Excuse me," he said, "There is one more item on the agenda that must be addressed." Mirsky gave him the floor. "We have become aware of some issues and actions that were taken which were not in the letter or spirit of our agreements. If such issues ever arise in the future, we will take them with the ultimate level of seriousness. That is all."

I felt like I had just gotten my driver's license back from the policeman, along with a warning instead of a ticket.

"Yes, we know," Mirsky said, "And we agree completely with our partner, Urobank. It will not happen again. Let's all go get something to eat."

As we walked out of the conference room, I heard a small comment from one of the Walton team, our regional leasing director. He was in the middle of his own personal issues, trying to move his family to the United Kingdom from Poland, and I am sure he had little interest in becoming more entwined in our Russian problems. He was also highly regarded by Urobank for his work in Poland and probably saw little personal gain in undermining that relationship. He had also, quite clearly in my eyes, moved physically away from me at the beginning of that day, lest some of my misfortunes rub off. He walked close by me on our way out the door, smiled, and said, "Remarkable recovery."

With the board meeting over, I headed home to Chicago in early August for a few weeks of vacation, as well as some resolution and absolution from the Walton home office. Two weeks after the board meeting I was in the Walton office when Robert Goldman came in and asked if I was following what was going on with the Russian stock market. "I'm on vacation," I said, "so no."

"Better look," he said. "And call them."

On August 13, the Russian stock market seized up and the next day the ruble fell against the dollar from 6 to 7.4. I called our office on Friday, August 14, and told them to sell all rubles immediately. They said it was too late in the day and easier to do on Monday. On Monday, the exchange rate was already 8.0. We lost about $20,000 on that exchange, but the rest of our company funds were held in US dollars. There was some kind of reason why my Russian staff said selling the rubles could wait, but it struck all of us that they were not sufficiently serious about what was going on. When I got back to St. Petersburg on August 24, the ruble began a second and much greater slide, hitting double digits, past 12.0. The news in general was not reassuring for any banks, so on August 31 I emptied all of the Walton-Petersburg

US dollar accounts and wired the funds to Chicago. Technically, I had local signature authority, but I was supposed to request internal authorization from Chicago before I could exercise it. In an e-mail to our accountant in Chicago I stated simply—and, of course, sarcastically—that I knew I should have waited for his okay, so if he wanted to, he had every right to send all the money back to Russia.

Really, what I thought at the start of the formal Russian financial crisis in August 1998 was something like, so what? After what I had gone through personally—which had been, like most things in life, partly or mainly my own fault—I felt like I had already passed through the process of "dying unto one's self," what Joseph Campbell describes as the critical moment in a classical myth. So I figured that nothing else was going to faze me. Anyway, how much worse could it get?

CHAPTER 10

EXIT VISAS

"A man capable of telling my wife that she cannot
get on that plane has not yet been born."

The crisis tore like a wildfire through the emerging Russian economy. It bankrupted Britansky Dom and we lost all of our retail tenants. In October, BHS met with us and calmly told us they couldn't pay their rent. They had been making progress at turning things around, selling off inventory with new sales, looking for new fashions, but the crisis knocked them out with a perfect one-two punch. First, it froze all their funds in the bank, many, I believe, in rubles that were suddenly worth 25 percent of what they had been. Then it obliterated the small emerging middle class that was their target customer base. Body blow and then an upper cut to the chin. They were out.

After meeting with us in our offices, BHS held a meeting in the atrium and told their employees they would all lose their jobs. There was a lot of silence and some crying. We called our attorneys and started to examine our options. BHS still owed us a lot of money and we couldn't let them walk away with all of their merchandise, so we simply seized their goods as being abandoned, using the same legal argument we had used for dealing with Special Health Care's furniture. Then we tried to figure out how to settle with BHS.

I instructed our staff to videotape the process of removing every item from the store and locking it in the storage area we had set aside on the vacant fourth floor. I didn't want any question of our stealing any of the goods. The tape would be our insurance and our evidence if we ever wound up in a court. The staff did as I requested. A few days later I asked for the video.

"It's a continuous video," the head guard said.

"So give it to me so we can keep it safe," I answered.

"It's continuous," he repeated. "We did videotape everything as you asked, but then the next day we taped over it."

I didn't know what to say. I had seen the movie *The Gang That Couldn't Shoot Straight* and felt like we were auditioning but failing to make the callback. We were not sure how BHS would respond to our seizure of their goods, and wondered if they would consider sending their own guards to simply take it all back. A day later I walked out of our building and was more than a little surprised to see that the front doors were gone.

"Where are the doors?" I asked the guards at the reception area.

"Oh, we have finally gotten Kemalco to fix those scratches from the punch list," they answered.

"Do you think now is the best time for our building not to have any front doors?" I asked.

"We have a guard here twenty-four hours, so we should be fine."

Why not?

The crisis impacted everyone I knew. A British expat of Russian descent with long family ties to St. Petersburg had formed his own real-estate agency and had no idea how he was going to survive. His bank accounts were all in rubles, and he told me as he walked down the main shopping street, he tried to figure out what he could do with his rubles to keep them from disappearing. Could he buy television sets and store them as a hedge against inflation? His accounts were locked up and he couldn't buy dollars. Everything he had worked for to get his business off the ground, returning to Russia, the country of his grandparents, and reforming a family business, was now going down the toilet faster and faster.

As for my own family, it had been clear since August that we would be leaving Russia. We began to plan a fighting retreat. For me this meant how to replace Britansky Dom. For my wife it meant having the right to leave in the first place, since her visa had expired and she had applied for a special journalist's visa that would give her almost diplomatic status.

There was pressure for me to leave St. Petersburg from a Walton perspective, for the simple reason that I was now just overhead and not a source of revenue. We had been paid a development fee—and collected every dollar due—to complete the development, which had been tied to the completion of the construction contract for the base building. We earned some fees for construction oversight of the tenant improvement works, and property-management fees to cover Nikolai's salary, but my salary was a little gray. Walton also wanted me in Warsaw to help with our new projects there.

Before the crisis, we had started to pursue a high-rise office project in Moscow that would be a bank headquarters. Walton had brought the Russian bankers to St. Petersburg to show that we had a Russian presence, and then took them to Warsaw to show them the type of high-rise structure we would build in Moscow. Once the crisis hit, this kind of development became out of the question. Russian banks were among the hardest hit, and there was no international financing eager to enter Russia when the government itself was defaulting on loans.

I would have wanted to go to Moscow to get some step-up recognition, but I probably would not have been given the professional responsibilities I was looking for. This would have led either to disappointment or further growth, if I stepped into a role greater than my initial assignment, as I had in St. Petersburg. Seeing how crazy I had become working on the smaller project in St. Petersburg, my wife told me bluntly that she did not think our marriage would survive another Russian project. I would have found it almost impossible to say no to a new challenge if I had been asked to go. In that sense, the crisis saved us from having that argument and might have saved our marriage—at least for another twelve years. We began to plan the move to Poland.

Roger Glass was very supportive. After the July board meeting, he had asked me how I liked being in Russia, and I told him that living in Russia was like sitting in a leaky tent. It drips on your head and it bugs you. You put up with it because you have other things to think about, but then one day you decide, "The hell with it! I am fixing the leak."

It's not that big a deal to fix a leaking tent. You could get a patch, a new tarp, or even another tent. But as soon as you start sewing on a patch, some asshole appears from nowhere and asks what you're doing and whether you have a permit. No, you answer, it's my tent and I'm fixing it. Well, you need a permit. And you need a local company, and ... and ... and ... So soon you decide that fixing the leak just isn't worth it. The leak is easy, but the permits and the interference are without end. Glass told me later that he understood from that conversation that it was time for me to leave.

Our move from Russia was always going to be toward more normal, not toward more challenging. Even the Russians call the hinterland outside of Moscow or St. Petersburg the *glubinki* (depths). When Allan was in charge, Ralph and others had been approached about even more exotic locations for the company's next building. Why not Azerbaijan? The Stans! Allan had already been dealing with unhappy employees and their various expat family problems on the ground.

"The Stans," he said. "Which Stan would that be? Kazakhstan? Kyrgyzstan? How about Make-a-New-Plan Stan or I-Quit Stan?" He told them to forget about finding employees to go to the Stans and to instead focus on the projects we had in hand.

Before I took the job with Walton, I had sketched an arc on a scrap of paper. The arc led from Bulgaria to Russia and then back home to Chicago. As with any developer, that doodle stuck in

my head and was actually locked in my brain as the master plan
for our whole time overseas. So when Walton suggested I go to
Moscow, I said sure, if I can be more of a development executive.
But if the idea is that I become the "Russian" expert to support a
senior development expert, then no. I told them I didn't want to
be the best rattlesnake killer on the frontier. I wanted to learn a
trade that would be worthwhile back in the United States.

"The States!" Ralph replied. "Back in the States people like
you are a dime a dozen. We need you here in Europe!"

One fact I had locked onto early in my expat career was that
unhappy spouses were the reason for 75 percent of all employees leaving their positions. So finding a way to keep your spouse
happy and fulfilled was a key, perhaps the key, to long-term
employee commitments. Russia had been good to my wife and
her career since she could write about all of the crazy things
that happened, and there was an appetite in the *Chicago Tribune*
and *Wall Street Journal Europe* for her stories. She had worked
diligently even after Charlie was born to connect with the various newspapers that hired freelance writers, and had become
a sponsored stringer for several publications. She had a nice
group of journalist friends based mostly in Moscow. She had
a lot of guts too, learning enough Russian to get by and going
off by herself or with a translator to places like the Caucuses to
interview Cossacks, and to Tallinn, Riga, and nearby cities such
as Novgorod.

My position helped her in several ways, not least of which
she was able to cut through the PR nonsense that was a line of
defense for many expats. She had teased one Spanish company

owner about his permits. "Aren't you supposed to fly these people to Spain for research?" she asked. "We did, we did!" he said. "But they still didn't give us the permit."

The Internet was just becoming a key business tool more than the fax, and no country was more advanced or more ready to accept the new technology than the twenty-year-old leaders of Estonia. One night, after my wife had secured an assignment to write about Tallinn, the capital of Estonia, she was researching the president of Estonia and trying to figure out how to get an interview with him. With a population of only 1.5 million people, it should have been possible, but with traditional layers of bureaucracy, it could also have been impossible. It was 1:00 a.m. and the baby was sleeping, so she had some free time, and there it was on the president's website, a link to speak to the president. *Why not?* she thought, and wrote asking for an interview, apologizing for the unorthodox and impolite manner of an e-mail past midnight.

"Not impolite at all," came the e-mailed response at 1:30 a.m., from the president himself. "I'll have my secretary contact you tomorrow."

We had been dealing successfully with visas for years. The multientry visa was a key element in getting to stay and work in Russia. I had pushed early on for the Atrium company to establish a contract with MEA (Ministry for External Affairs) so that we had privileges to secure entry visas within twenty-four hours. We were leasing a Class A building to international tenants. The dumbest thing in the world would be for our tenants and their various executives or consultants not to be able to get into Russia to see the actual building in person. Multientry visas were harder to get but necessary if you lived and worked in Russia. These visas were good for six months, meaning we needed to leave the country and reenter every six months. The logical thing for my family was to organize trips to Finland, about three hours away. That also enabled me to renew the temporary import status on my car.

Ever since I first went to Russia in the 1980s, Finland was a kind of recovery zone for me, like Wiesbaden for US troops returning home. When my student program was over in 1981 and I had blown through all of my money with Finnish friends, I arrived late at the Helsinki airport with only $5 in my wallet. I missed the plane and figured I would be sleeping in a chair at the terminal. Instead, Finnair decided the missed connection was their fault. They paid me 25 percent of the cost of my round-trip ticket—about $200—and gave me vouchers for a night in a four-star hotel, a steak dinner, and a shuttle bus to the hotel. I felt like Odysseus near the end of his journeys when he washed ashore naked on an island, and was clothed and fed by the local king before he finally returned to Ithaca. Helsinki was also where I first discovered kiwi, and I marveled at how the capitalist system could ship this fruit all the way from New Zealand without a blemish, while just next door in the Soviet Union, tomatoes couldn't travel five miles without getting destroyed.

When we worked in Russia in the 1990s, Lisa and I even took our dog with us to Finland.

"You need this, you need that," the old functionaries at the Finnish border harped when we interrupted their Russian version of *Columbo* late one winter night. "Rabies certificate, health certificate, birth certificate, blah blah blah."

"Hold on," I said. "Let me get the dog to show you."

Griffin had blue eyes, and every Russian who saw them fell in love with him immediately. So I brought in our rambunctious Australian shepherd, and he jumped up at the ladies.

"*Golubiye glaziey!*" they screamed in unison. "Oh, so cute, my *masinka*, my *lubimaya*. Oh, oh, oh."

He was licking their faces. So much for the birth certificate.

But the journalist visa was outside of my purview. And Lisa wanted to get it for herself as a form of validation. She didn't want a visa as my wife, the trailing spouse. She wanted that multiyear journalist visa, which would not only result in discounted trains and such, but would help her gain access to certain official events. So she started the visa process, which was a nightmare and involved many trips to Moscow.

Sometimes when I went to Moscow for Atrium business, I wound up delivering in person some document or other item related to her visa to the MEA office in Moscow.

"He needs a bottle of Scotch or he won't give you the paper," I was told once.

Whatever, I thought, and the next time I was in a duty-free store while on a trip, I saw just what I needed, Passport Scotch. I thought this was actually kind of clever and appropriate. The Moscow official was not amused. He said, "Next time, Johnny Walker."

That was actually my third or fourth attempt to pick up the Moscow paper that I needed to give to the local office in

St. Petersburg. The Moscow-based bureaucrat was a first-class prick. He kept inventing new hurdles and delighted in watching how upset his applicants became. "Don't tell me how much of a jerk I am," he explained one time to my wife. "When I lived in Germany in the 1980s, the Germans were awful to me, so now it is simply my turn in life to be awful to someone else." How edifying.

When the official was finally ready to give me the paper I needed, he said we could meet at a Soviet-era bar in Moscow. When I walked into the dark bar, he invited me for a drink at my expense. As he walked up to the bar to order, he casually made a backhand toss of the envelope with my permission in it onto an empty table. *Asshole*, I thought. *He knows what that envelope means to me and he is deliberately doing that.* I had a drink and talked about nothing, and then I opened the envelope and made sure it had the right name on it. Step one done.

Back in St. Petersburg, I asked Katya, my assistant at Walton whom I had hired to replace Tatiana, to help Lisa navigate the local MEA office. The MEA office was an endless source of silliness, designed somehow to work as badly as possible. For example, the fees—less than $10—could only be paid at a certain local bank, which the authorities must have paced off so that they knew it took thirty minutes to get there and another thirty minutes to get back. Given the small opening hours of the MEA office, it was literally impossible to pick up an invoice at the MEA office, go to the bank, pay the fee, and return to the MEA the same day. That would have been an outrage. So the simplest thing took several days and often a week.

My first year in Russia I had dutifully wasted weeks getting my own visa properly registered at this same office. Enough. The next year I learned that a local hotel would provide the same stamp to nonguests for 20 dollars. Five minutes. Much better. Unfortunately, for Lisa's type of visa, she had to follow the formal system. "For my friends, anything," the Italians say. "For my enemies, the law."

"You know," our Atrium secretary said as the days went by and our departure date drew nearer with no resolution to Lisa's visa in sight, "they won't let her on the plane if she doesn't have the visa to leave."

I just laughed. "A man capable of telling my wife she cannot get on that plane has not yet been born."

Lisa went countless times to the MEA office with Katya and engaged in countless Monty-Pythonesque exchanges with the nasty lady who ran the office. Finally, one day when the head lady was not there, they encountered a really nice clerk who promised to actually do something. A few weeks later they informed Lisa the visa was ready. Lisa and Katya went in to pick it up. Lisa had with her a large box, gift wrapped and with a big bow on it. She walked into the office and met with the head bitch that had been such a problem.

First she set the package on her desk, and the woman, brightening, could not keep her eyes from wandering back and forth from the papers in front of her to the box. "You see," the woman said, "we have your visa. It doesn't take that long when you have all the right paperwork."

Lisa waited until the woman had stamped everything and handed Lisa the visa. Lisa then thanked her, picked up the present, and asked the woman where her assistant sat, the one who had helped her so much. Lisa then walked calmly away from the desk as the face of the head clerk reddened.

"You should not have done that," Katya said as they left the office. "You know that you can never come back to this office ever again."

"Fine with me," Lisa said.

Russians are funny. They rail against the system they live in, but they know that they have to live with it, so they are a lot less aggressive than an American. An American will think, this system is ridiculous and I am not going to put up with it. System be damned.

Still Russians have their own ways. A Russian colleague asked me one day, "Do you know the last act of a Russian emigrating from his country once he walks across the border? He turns around and spits."

CHAPTER 11

THE GRANDFATHER PART II

"Today we settle all family business"
"What the heck is a Grinch?"

At the closing of the project in November 1996, I was made general director and Kleptov demoted to assistant director, as part of the deal to close the financing. The given reason was the failure of the bank where the company had purchased a million-dollar CD. Kleptov wasn't to blame for that decision, but he took it in the neck anyway as a sacrificial scapegoat.

Freed from his distractions, we made great progress with the development. We opened the building and moved into our management office. In the new office, I hired Nikolai to be the property manager. This left the position of assistant director somewhat superfluous. So Kleptov was free to pursue all his extracurricular projects; but unfortunately, I still needed his cosignature to send wire transfers to pay our bills. I got completely sick of going into his office and listening to his latest silliness as a price for paying our bills.

In the summer of 1998, Greg C., our attorney in DC, called to say that we were behind in paying our bills and that if we didn't catch up, he would need to stop working on our project. We were finally rolling on the leasing of the remaining space in the building—the number one priority for all of the company partners—and the idea that we would lose the services of our key attorney was just beyond. I was sure we had paid since I had signed the payment forms a week earlier. But then Maya told me that all of the payment forms had backed up on Kleptov's desk.

I stormed into Kleptov's small private office and closed the door. His sole window had been decorated with enough papers to block any view by the other staff. The small locked safe he had taken with him from our apartment office sat under the desk next to his legs.

"Look at this fax," I said. "Look at the time stamp when this lease was sent to me. It was midnight in Washington, DC. That means that Greg worked until midnight his time to get this lease done. Then I worked on the revisions on our end and sent it back to him. We are using the eight-hour time difference perfectly, so as soon as we go to sleep, he wakes up and vice versa. All working smoothly so we can lease this space. What the hell is your problem?"

"Please sit down," he said. "I know we have to pay the bills, but I want to ask you something. The employees, for their health-care insurance, need a place for rest and relaxation, so I was wondering if maybe we could get a company condominium in Spain for them to use."

I can't even describe how off-the-wall this sounded. We had finished our development by the skin of our teeth in terms of our budget, and we still needed to finish all of the tenant improvements. We were also in the middle of a financial crisis. "A condo in Spain?" I asked. "*What?*"

"Well," continued Kleptov, "it turns out I already have a condo in Spain that I sold to the developer there when I traded up. I sold it and gave them $20,000."

"Grigory, I'm losing the translation here. When you sell something, you get money. When you buy something, you give money. What did you do, sell or buy?"

"Well, both. I sold a small condo and bought a larger one."

"So now you want Krasotsky 23 to buy out your condo investment in Spain. Grigory, this is insane. We need to pay the fucking legal bills. And the other bills, the architects, etc. No condo, no health insurance, just the bills, the ones in the budget, the ones we need to pay to finish the building."

I never learned how to translate *fucking* into Russian, but I was sure he understood the English word in the middle of my Russian sentence.

The other bill I will never forget was the one for lightbulbs. One thousand dollars for lightbulbs. To this day, I still have never seen an invoice like the one that was presented to me for signature one day. Base price for lightbulbs—$500; tax—$100; profit on the lightbulbs—$100; delivery—$100; the income tax the company had to pay on the lightbulb sale—$200. Total—$1,000.

I took the bill to Kleptov. "Grigory, can you please sit with me for a minute?" I asked. "Grigory, does this invoice with your signature on it seem normal to you?"

"Oh, yes, it's a good company."

"Grigory, I have never in my life paid someone else's income tax on their marked-up profit on a sale. Grigory, that's crazy. And so is paying $1,000 for lightbulbs. I am keeping this invoice in my records, and if I ever see anything like this again, I am going to give it to the board of directors."

⚛

"If I go, I can't leave him in charge," I told Ralph on one of his visits in the fall of 1998. "We've made such a beautiful building, made so many sacrifices. I'd prefer to just blow it up myself all at once rather than let him slowly destroy it."

"I get it," Ralph said. "Does Mirsky know what he's up to?"

"I don't know. That's something I never broached. But they're Russian. They must know."

"Okay, let us handle it. You do your job."

My job had two main issues at that point. Finish construction of the tenant improvements for Regus Business Centers, which had leased our entire second floor, about 20 percent of the building; and find a way to resolve the loss of BHS, which had turned our entire first floor dark and was the most visible sign of our problems. We were hardly alone with problems as the crisis unfolded, but that empty retail space created a terrible image that was easily visible to the entire city.

The Regus construction was working itself out. Our Russian subcontractor, Pace, was proceeding on schedule to complete the interior improvements in time for us to gain a few thousand dollars in bonus and, more importantly, avoid big penalties in lost rent if we were late. Regus owed us a large advance-rental payment, due on the day they moved in. I had agreed with Slova that if we collected the Regus advance payment, the Atrium company would approve the reimbursement of Walton's fees for my staying in St. Petersburg for another year after the completion of the base building. It was about $125,000.

"Eyes on the prize," I had told Roger Glass when I said I was getting a lot done in Russia.

He looked at me like I was an imbecile. "What prize is there in Russia?" he asked.

"$125,000," I said. Roger was a big supporter, but he didn't seem convinced that I knew what I was talking about.

As the crisis continued to unfold, the ruble declined wildly, ultimately reaching 25 rubles to the dollar, less than 25 percent of its value in August. The sluggish banking system made it impossible to make payments in rubles, which was required according to the law. Contracts were written in US dollars, but payment had to be made in the equivalent amount of rubles. In a functioning system, this would not be an issue, but because the banks and the system were subject to seizures, no one could guarantee how long a transfer would take to process. If it took several days and the ruble fell in the meantime, what left my account as $100 might arrive in your account as $60, or not arrive at all. It was too risky to make such payments, but something had to be done.

So the head of Pace, Sasha Celsky, came to me one day with a plan. "We have been forming groups," he said, "of people we can trust with accounts in the same banks as we have. Instead of sending money between banks, we are making transfers within a bank that are balanced by similar transfers at other banks."

It reminded me of how Wall Street started, with people standing on the curb in the 1700s. So I asked him what his proposal was.

"Well, you owe us $320,000, and we need the money to pay for the Regus construction. We have a group that we trust who has an account in your bank and an account in ours. If you pay them $200,000 and then $120,000, we will give you an acceptance note for the same amount against your construction contract."

"What am I actually paying for?"

"Meat in Tatarstan."

"Sasha, are you sure about this?"

"Yes. I know these people. If you get the release on the same amount, what does it matter how you actually make the payment? Look, we will agree on boundaries for the exchange rate. Today it seems stable at 15, so let's say anything less than 16 is fine for tomorrow. We'll call in the morning to see the official rate, and if it is within this range, then the trade will go through."

"Okay," I said. "Let's do it."

He was right, of course. If I received his official receipt for the money, applying it to our construction contract, then I didn't care if I was buying meat in Tatarstan or paying for drywall in St. Petersburg. There was no need, however, to mention it to Urobank or our board. They just wanted to know if the Regus construction was proceeding on schedule, to which I could answer yes.

The next morning, October 5, the ruble *strengthened* to 12 rubles to the dollar. "The trade is off," Sasha said. "Something is wrong. We don't know how the ruble has gotten stronger. Everyone is nervous."

I didn't get it either. Was the crisis over somehow? Hardly. Later we learned that the Russian Central Bank had intervened. It had bought rubles, using its limited reserves to drive the value up so that the trigger pricing on certain bonds would be more favorable. It was then that I realized how small a fish we were in this market, where the government itself was manipulating the currency to help certain players.

A week later the currency settled into its pattern of more predictable decline. The trade went through, and Regus continued on its way.

But what to do about Britansky Dom? One day two Finnish businessmen, Ilka and Jorma, asked to see us. "We see you have a problem," they said, looking at the dark retail space. "We have a problem too, and we think we should talk."

They explained that they represented Stockmann, the largest department store in Finland. Nearly nine months earlier they had ordered a massive quantity of merchandise to ship to their new Moscow store, which was opening in time for Christmas. But the financial crisis guaranteed that they would never sell all of this merchandise, which was already in motion and couldn't be stopped. So what to do? Maybe, they thought, they could spread the merchandise around.

They came to see us in mid-October. We had a bankrupt store with seized merchandise and no settlement of any kind with our existing tenant. Our potential tenant wanted to be open for Christmas with a new store, newly registered and so forth, in less than nine weeks. The Russian Christmas is in January, but the buying season starts in December. In Russia, it is said, "Nothing and everything is possible (*Nichevo i vsyo vozmozhno*)." We, of course, went for the deal.

We had enjoyed an extremely high rental rate with our bankrupt tenant, and the rate was fixed. The Finns wanted a percentage lease, which we knew would be a problem if there was no fixed payment of any kind, so we negotiated a floor and got approval from our lenders. We tried to convince the Russian partners of the merits of a percentage lease, but at first they were highly skeptical.

"They won't give us the true sales figures," our partners said.

"They are Finns," I said. "And we'll get audited statements from a CPA in Helsinki and copies of monthly sales reports."

When Kleptov heard about the proposed terms, he began contacting other Russian firms to see if they could also make a proposal for a percentage deal.

Five weeks later I was on a plane to Helsinki to finalize the lease agreement. I still didn't have board approval to sign it, but I didn't think it necessary to tell the Finns that. We had to move forward, and it would be easier to get final approval on my side if I showed the board a signed lease. I just made up some excuse for not signing as we went through the final details. After I left the attorney's office, I took a plane to Lappeenranta at midnight, where I had to transfer to a small jump plane for the final journey. It was December and so cold outside. The shiny lights on the fog-shrouded tarmac reminded me of the last scene in *Casablanca*. I walked through the small duty-free store and picked up something to drink. I don't remember what, probably Lapin Kulta beers. The propeller plane took off, and when we had landed and I had taken a taxi back to our apartment, the first thing I did before drinking the beer was to get on the AOL account using our dial-up connection and send a one-line e-mail to Walton in Chicago, where it would have been midafternoon.

"Krasotsky 23 is 65% leased again."

But we weren't exactly leased, because technically the space still belonged to the bankrupt Britansky Dom company. More to the point, we needed BHS's help to open the Stockmann store. The antitheft devices couldn't be imported from Finland in time for the opening, so we needed to borrow fixtures and the antitheft devices from BHS. And I couldn't exactly tell BHS that we really needed their help, because that would skew the negotiations.

So I went to Moscow, where Neel Mahatra—the senior advisor for the BHS franchisee—had just returned from India. We met in a bar, where I was already talking with a journalist who was giving me $300 to pass on to my wife to pay her for one of her stories. "Don't say a word," I told Neel. "He is a journalist." I introduced Neel as an old friend, and after one beer the journalist took off.

Neel and I started to talk, and Neel laughed like a wise old man. "What have you and Hassan done?" he asked, chuckling and shaking his head. "What have you and Hassan done?"

"Well," I started to respond indignantly, "we—" I wanted to say, "Well, *he started it!*"

"What kind of mess have you made?" he continued, still laughing. "How are we going to fix this?"

BHS had their own problems in Moscow, and more importantly with their own lenders. They could have taken us to arbitration, but they wanted a settlement as quickly as possible to avoid triggering cross defaults with their other financers. Our attorney Greg had guessed this, and he had told me recently before we began a conference call with BHS: *"Don't laugh. I mean it. My response to every suggestion they make is going to be about the arbitrator, and if you laugh it will ruin it. So don't laugh."*

I kept quiet on the call. Greg did exactly as he said, and his answer to every question was, "Well, if the arbitrator wants to agree today is Friday, then ..." Finally they gave up and ended the call. That was a week before I met Neel in the bar.

"What are you going to do with the merchandise?" Neel asked. "You aren't a retailer. You don't have the right or the permissions to sell it. Give it back to us."

"It's all there," I insisted, forgetting for a minute about the video fiasco. "It's all locked up, and it's dry and it's safe. And no, we don't want it. We want to be paid and we want to try to release the space. We might be able to release at least some of it ..."

We began to sketch out a settlement, and as we drafted it later I added in requests about the fixtures staying in place so we wouldn't ruin the walls. What would they do with the shelves anyway, and this would save them the cost of restoring the walls to their preleased state. The last thing I asked for as an aside was the security devices. I never told them until the last minute that we had a deal with Stockmann. Secretly, I had even considered trying to reuse the facade letters. You could actually spell *Stokman* in Russian with the letters from *Britansky Dom*, and they were both dark green in color, but the Stockmann people didn't take my proposal seriously at all.

At the board meeting to approve the lease deal, Kleptov first asked for a chance to present his alternative proposal for a local company to pay a higher percentage than Stockmann was paying—wow, how did they know what percentage to bid?—but the writing was already on the wall and Mirsky's patience was less than thin. "We accept this deal from the Finns," he said, "but we would never in a million years accept this kind of deal from your partners. Let's move on."

With the lease deal signed and the settlement being finalized, everyone flew into action. Mirsky gave the command to get things done, and the local team jumped. All of the engineers worked to make the connections, and we got Pace involved in any light construction. Stockmann actually rehired the BHS head manager and a number of the staff, who already knew the building and its systems.

We had one final problem. The telephone system. We had a PBX (private branch exchange), which gave us an exclusive in the building. Kleptov saw it as a kind of gold mine, where we could force tenants to pay high rates for high-quality phone service as if they were captive guests in a hotel. In real life the availability of high-quality phone service was a requirement, but we could never force the retail tenants to use our system. Their data requirements were more sophisticated than our small PBX system could handle. Each purchase sent information to the accounting department in Helsinki and to the warehouse tracking inventory somewhere else. Our PBX wasn't compatible, and we decided early on that we were in the real-estate business, not the phone business. This was like a classic MBA case study—selling beef versus selling cowhides. Kleptov was angry but too bad. I never liked the phone business.

There was another problem on the Finnish side. Stockmann's IT department told them that the four-week timeframe was too short and it simply couldn't be done.

Jorma had negotiated the deal and was furious. He told me he stormed into their IT offices in Helsinki. "You people," he screamed, *"nobody knows what you do!* Everyone is working hard to get this done. Even the *Russians* are on schedule! But you, *you* are the only ones who say it can't be done. Get to work!"

In my experience, Finns don't usually speak this way, especially to one another, so I could see how this would have made an impact.

On December 15, Stockmann opened their store and the lights went back on for Krasotsky 23. We had a big reception, but I left before the serious drinking because we had made plans to meet with Lyuba's family. I was caught up in the spirit of the season, and I was also desperate to be home on Christmas vacation and to show two-year-old Charlie our *How the Grinch Stole Christmas!* video back in our apartment in Chicago. Lisa had finally secured her exit visa, and we were more than ready to go home. My quote in an article in the local English-language paper was simple: "This Grinch of a crisis will not stop Christmas from coming to Krasotsky 23."

"*Shto takoe* Grinch?" Slova asked me. ("What the heck is a Grinch?") They had translated the article for Mirsky, and no one on their team could find *grinch* in any dictionary. I tried to explain it was a character in a children's cartoon that every American would know.

After the December board meeting, Mirsky, Ralph, and Diana called for a private meeting with Kleptov. I was not invited but heard later what had been said. Mirsky said that the board was greatly disappointed that Krasotsky 23 had not collected the security deposit for BHS, and that after reflection, they had determined that this was Kleptov's responsibility as assistant director and therefore they were asking for his immediate resignation. Apparently Neptune had done its own recon on Kleptov's activities and discovered some problems. The stated crime, of course, was not his responsibility at all—it was clearly mine—but the Russian legal system is hard to follow sometimes. And Kleptov was hardly innocent, just not guilty of the particular transgression he had been charged with.

No matter, he was out. He was, as before, most nervous about his car. He had to give it back since he was leaving. "Why don't you just pay off the loan?" I suggested. The loan was originally made in rubles at 6 to the dollar, and the ruble was now 25 to the dollar, so the loan on his BMW could be paid off for about $5,000. Kleptov leaped at this suggestion and paid it off, but apparently when Mirsky found out, he was furious and it proved to be the final bridge burned. *Just as well,* I thought.

Alex Slova, the Komsomol scout counterpart to me as Eagle Scout, was appointed to take over. The most famous saying at the

University of Chicago Business School is: There is no free lunch. Slova told me the Russian equivalent: The only free cheese is in the mouse trap. Sometimes we really were on the same page.

On the morning before I left Russia, Slova and I drove to the Finnish border so we could "export" the company Saab in my name and "import" it back in his name. The orange sun in the white sky is truly beautiful, even though it barely breaks the horizon at that time of year. We drove through the no-man's-land between the Russian and Finnish customs booths, took off the Finnish plates, made a U-turn, wrote a one-page contract, and registered the car at the Russian border in his name.

Regus had paid their rent, and the last thing Slova did before I left St. Petersburg was to wire $125,000 to Walton in Chicago. "A signature is a signature," he said. "A deal is a deal." It floored our US partner when the money arrived.

The next day I went to the airport. Our possessions had been moved out of our apartment and piled up in one of the vacant offices at Krasotsky 23, pending customs clearance to send them to Poland. We took all of our Russian coins to the fountain in the middle of the atrium and had Charlie toss them in. There were a lot of coins. We thought it was cute, but the people sitting at the atrium café looked at us like we were friends of Marie Antoinette, being gauche in the middle of the crisis.

We said our good-byes and flew home to Chicago. When we arrived on December 20, we walked across the street and bought a Christmas tree from the church lot. Then I took Charlie upstairs to the third-floor loft of our condo, where our television and video were set up, plugged in the Grinch video, and sat him on my lap. The music started, playing the famous song I had waited to hear, as the Whos down in Whoville gathered around their holiday tree.

"Fahoo fores dahoo dores, Welcome Christmas bring your light …"

We did it.

EPILOGUE:
TOYLKO DOVERIYE
("ONLY TRUST")

Connecticut Capital (CT), our financial partner at Walton, had been floored when the money arrived. "Awesome" was the comment scribbled across my e-mail and faxed back to me. They had never expected anything like that from Russia, which they had almost universally written off. In January 1999, I went to a meeting in Warsaw with CT, where a Walton colleague, who soon after left Walton to head a new firm called TRI-MI-BM, was making a brief presentation on his most recent business development efforts with one of the Russian oligarchs.

"We were off the coast of Iraq," he began, "drinking on a speedboat called *Octapussy*—"

"Stop!" the CT representative said. "I think … No, I *know* that I have heard enough to say we are not interested in anymore projects in Russia."

Not everyone, though, was pleased with the payment from Krasotsky 23 to Walton. EXPOC was furious. They had thought Walton should work for free since the Krasotsky company was in a holding pattern. Of course, our response was if that was their proposal, then they should find someone else to work for free in Russia, which would limit the supply of their potential project managers.

I had figured EXPOC would be pissed, but I had said to myself at the time that I couldn't keep playing both sides of the chess game. We had invited their staff to St. Petersburg to tour the site and review all of our financial projections, but after a few hours they had asked to see the famous palaces. So of course I arranged for them to see all of the special palaces, including my favorite Cottage Palace at Peterhof. Still, at some point it wasn't my job to do their job.

And one thing that EXPOC didn't ever seem to understand was that the Russians were not going to miss a loan payment. "I will not lose my face in this city," Mirsky had said as he walked out of a board meeting, and that sentiment applied to an international loan. By seemingly grouping all of the Russians together, EXPOC didn't understand that there are lots of different kinds of Russians, just like there are different kinds of Americans. Not everyone is an Eagle Scout, and even they can make mistakes.

I flew to Washington, DC, to meet with EXPOC in March 1999. The Atrium was moving along, back toward normal. I was based in Poland, but really spending all of my time trying to redo what we had already done in St. Petersburg. I sat alone in a conference room of the EXPOC office on New Jersey Avenue, waiting. It was starting to snow, and I knew that soon the whole city would empty out in a panic as the forecast reached the terrible one-inch mark.

The door opened and they marched in, all in a line. There were about six people, if I remember correctly. They had clearly all been together, because they all arrived at the same time. It was a show of force. *Silly force,* I thought. What do you need six people for? I always thought that when you need lots of people, you probably don't feel very confident in your position. So I smiled to myself. What else could I do anyway? I hadn't brought any money; and they needed to understand what we were doing in St. Petersburg.

I tried to explain. No, we weren't going to fire anyone. Neptune, the 40 percent owner of the project, had gotten involved in the first place to provide jobs for former naval officers in the submarine program. All of the cleaning and maintenance engineers were from the Neptune family of workers. All of the guards were former officers. Russia was in a deep crisis and there was no way that Mirsky, as padrone of his submarine group, was going to toss some of his people out on the street. Their salaries weren't that big anyway, so this wasn't the issue.

"Come to Russia," I said, "and see for yourself what we are doing."

So EXPOC sent a representative in April. He arrived fresh from a meeting with some Siberian oil company that had also borrowed money from EXPOC. He did not look well. I got the sense the Siberian firm had told him something like, "F—— off and get lost" when he asked about his loan. There was an article in the *Wall Street Journal* at that time about a Russian oligarch, who described the foreign lenders who had proposed settling up with their borrower for just five cents on the dollar. "They are suffocating in greed!" the oligarch responded. I knew our group would make a much better impression. But this representative hadn't come alone.

The Russian girl with him could not have been more than twenty years old. She may have been a distant relative, maybe a niece? Maybe not. More like men behaving badly. He asked me if she could come on the tour of the building with Mirsky, our seventy-year-old chairman, a Hero of Red Labor. *Have you lost your mind?* I thought, and then quickly regained mine. The girl had blue fingernail polish and an outfit out of *Tiger Beat*, the teen magazine back in the States. She was pretty, like a high school senior. I didn't want to ask. I did think that if there was something not quite right, we should take advantage of the situation. "Don't say a word," I told Slova when I brought our lender and his escort upstairs to our office to start the Atrium tour. Russians have a wonderful way of keeping a straight face, like a NYC Port Authority cop. No reaction whatsoever.

After the tour and the discussion and our suggestions for a forbearance agreement and some adjustments to the loan terms, the EXPOC representative was visibly relieved. "It's very reasonable," he said. "We'll discuss it in Washington." It was reasonable. So much for the marching band I had encountered in the conference room back in DC.

As a company, Krasotsky 23 was not out of the woods by any means. Besides Britansky Dom, we had lost all of our other retail tenants to bankruptcy and needed to replace them. We got creative. We looked for more leasable areas. We had been forced to keep all of the historic stairwells, but we weren't using them. We closed one off and turned its hallway into a narrow jewelry store. Another stairwell had two fake windows facing the atrium. There was an empty space beneath that stairwell in the basement. "What if we put in a dumbwaiter?" we wondered. "Maybe we could rent a café in the atrium." I asked three people in the restaurant business what they thought of this idea. They all liked it. Tom got to work with Sasha on designs and a budget. One of the restaurant operators gave us a proposal.

I liked this guy a lot. He was smart, had a tremendous sense of humor, and got things done. He had solved my earlier crisis of the guards not being able to feed themselves. They ate lunch in one of his banquet rooms. And he had introduced me to Aquavit, a kind of vodka aged in oaken casks. To be fair, Kleptov had introduced him to me. He was an operator. We gave him the plan for the basement space and our leasable area calculation.

"Are you nuts?" he asked. "You want to charge me rent for working around brick walls that are six feet thick?"

It wasn't easy to adapt the modern US Building Owners and Managers Association (BOMA) system to a Russian historic building. We were pioneers. We did the best we could.

"I can't change the system approved by our lenders," I said, "but I tell you what. Maybe we'll just do a bad job noticing how many tables can fit in the designated area that you'll rent."

Done. We had a café. A really nice addition to our building, and inadvertently, an answer to the problem of where our tenants could smoke. Lots of Russians smoked. They were our clients. It's cold outside on the street. Our ventilation system didn't allow for tenants smoking in their offices, but with a nearly one-hundred-foot glass ceiling, the café in the atrium allowed people to sit and have coffee while their smoke drifted up without bothering anyone at all. Live and let live.

We moved out of our beautiful third-floor offices, where you could watch the colors of the atrium walls change from the sunlight, down to the former Alphagraphics space in the basement. It was a poor retail space and had only one advantage as an office. When you sat at the basement-level windows and looked up, you could see all the lovely legs of the Russian ladies walking down Krasotsky Prospect. Mirsky had loved the suggestion that we would sacrifice our own office to move downstairs. There is a famous Soviet story about a soldier, Matrosov, who throws himself in front of the enemy's gun to save his unit. "Well done," Mirsky said.

"We have another idea," I said, "that could bring in some extra income. Our atrium is beautiful. Now we have a café. Why don't we rent out the atrium for weddings?"

The Russian partners froze, but then began to speak loudly among themselves, like when we had proposed the ceramic tiles. We didn't get it. After some minutes, Mirsky waved his hands and the conversations stopped. It was a bad idea, he explained. "A Russian wedding party," he said, "always ends … badly."

I was no longer in charge at Krasotsky 23. I had designated Nikolai as the full-time Walton property manager, and I was simply providing oversight and assistance long-distance from Warsaw. Here was how the business worked, I explained. "Keep the tenants happy, collect the rent, send the money to Chicago." After my near firing the prior summer, I smiled when the accountant in Chicago told our property manager in Warsaw that he should learn to write reports like I did.

"I write terrible reports," I said to Nikolai, "but every time I send anything to Chicago, I always send them some income from the project." I figured they didn't read the reports. They just noticed that instead of a funding request like others sent, I sent them money. Nice reports.

The workouts and renegotiations dragged on. As soon as the financial crisis had started, the US consulate asked us to reduce their rent or they would leave, citing the unconditional cancellation clause standard in their US government lease language.

"Wait a minute," I said. "When we were negotiating the lease, you promised that you would never, *ever* use that clause just to gain a commercial advantage. We asked for limitations, but you said that wasn't the purpose of the clause and you would never use it that way. Now you are first in line."

"Sorry," their manager said. "That's just the way it is."

"But the US government, meaning EXPOC, is our lender, so how can we pay the US government as a lender if the US government as a tenant doesn't want to pay their full rent?"

"Sorry," their manager said. "That's just the way it is."

So we played the same game as best we could. "We understand your request for lower rent," I said, "but our board meeting this month has been canceled, so we have to wait until our next meeting, which will be in two months."

After a few months, the US consulate representative pulled me aside and asked me point blank, "Are you just stalling because the longer you stall, the more we pay in higher rent?"

I looked directly into his eyes and said, "We would never, *ever* do that."

But we paid our loan interest and never defaulted. I actually thought we had done a good job under terrible circumstances. Years later, I met a colleague whose company also had a loan from EXPOC. "EXPOC likes us," I told him sincerely. He was a close friend of mine from a long time ago. "No, they don't," he said with perfect honesty. Well, I thought, maybe they should, but apparently they didn't.

⚬━◆━⚬

I saw many of the other Atrium players later in different situations.

Neel came to Poland when he was looking to expand Mothercare, a BHS-affiliated retailer that he had also managed in Russia. Mothercare was a great fit for Russia where it is bad luck to buy baby items before the actual birth. That meant that while the new mother was still at the hospital, a tipsy new father would appear at the store with a pocket full of rubles, and be promptly met at the door by a salesgirl.

"I never knew you were almost fired," Neel said. "I'm sorry about that."

"You didn't create the world we lived in," I told him. "You were just playing the game as best you could. I have no bad feelings. Plus, you did help us clean up the mess."

After I left Walton, I tried once to introduce a Romanian project to Urobank for funding. It was one of the most ambitious mixed-use developments in the entire country, but Urobank was not sure they wanted to get involved with the local Romanian partners who were backing it. I flew to London to attend the meeting I had arranged, but had to turn around in fifteen minutes and fly back to Poland because my son had a medical emergency in Warsaw. That meeting wasn't successful, but the project ultimately went ahead. I was glad that Diana had agreed to arrange the Urobank meeting in the first place. It showed me we had moved on.

Kemalco continued to work in Russia and in St. Petersburg. I attended their groundbreaking for a new hockey stadium. In keeping with the Turkish tradition, they had slit the throat of a ram on the site to spill animal blood, so that human blood would be saved. It was supposed to bring good luck.

"Did you do this on our site?" I asked.

"Three times," he responded.

Lisa, Charlie, and I came back to Russia several times over the years to visit Lyuba and Tatiana, who had married and was raising her own sons at their dacha. When our second son, David, was born in 2004, we flew back so they could see him. They were amazed that such old people in their forties had been able to have another baby.

I saw Mirsky in the international headlines in 1999 when the Russian submarine *Kursk* sank in frigid Arctic waters. I understood he was the only one who would agree to take charge of the salvage operation, risking his reputation on something that was seen as almost certain to fail. But they succeeded.

And Walton won the FIABCI Prix d'Excellence in 2000 for the Atrium project, partly because we were somehow able to reconcile all of the various goals of the multinational partners in creating a modern Western office building in the emerging Russian market. The award was presented in London at the Guildhall, with long medieval trumpets blowing just like at a jousting tournament in a Bugs Bunny cartoon. I loved being there for that.

⚬━✦━⚬

In the meantime, Russia's economy began to recover. The devaluation that had wiped out bank accounts ultimately spurred local manufacturing. Before, there wasn't much difference between the cost of Russian beer and a Heineken. Now the Heineken cost four times more. It began to make sense to produce all kinds of consumer goods in-country. Two factors improved the government's own finances. The world price of oil increased, generating more revenues; and the government instituted a flat 13 percent income tax, a rate so reasonable that most Russians decided that it no longer made any sense to play all of the games required to avoid income taxes. It was easier just to pay them.

In August 2000, I left Walton to take a position with PricewaterhouseCoopers in Warsaw. Before leaving I made one final trip to St. Petersburg, to deliver one last bottle of Scotch and to say good-bye to everyone, to Slova, to Nikolai, to Lyuba and Tatiana, to Sasha Celsky, and to Mirsky.

Slova had explained to me about the latest round of problems they had to deal with. Some city official had declared our land lease—basically our title—invalid because the lease had specified 6,000 square meters, the size of the original building, rather than 8,000 square meters, the size of the new building.

"So the whole thing was a trick?" I asked. "Once we completed the $30 million building, the lease would become legally invalid?" It was pure nonsense, but not out of the ordinary.

"We convinced him," Slova said, "that it was a mistake, yes, but since he was the landlord, it was his mistake because it is the landlord's responsibility to register the lease. No bureaucrat ever wants to accept personal responsibility. Once the official realized that the 'fault' was his, he fixed the problem immediately."

"*Kto vinovat?* (Who is guilty?)" I muttered. "Why do you do that? Why do Russians always have to know who is guilty before you do anything?"

Slova just shrugged and smiled. "We feel better," he said.

"By the way," I continued, "whatever happened next door, between the church and the Museum of Atheism?"

Years earlier, during construction, we had tried to make a deal on renting the parking lot at the Kazan Cathedral next door. Kleptov didn't know who to make the deal with. There was an ownership dispute between the Orthodox Church, which insisted the property belonged to the church since it had always been the central cathedral for St. Petersburg; and the Museum of Atheism, which had been established in the building by the Soviet authorities. Whoever owned the building, it seemed like an achievable goal to access their underutilized parking lot. But we couldn't make headway with either group. The museum had asked for too much rent, and the church felt it would be a sacrilege that would interfere with Orthodox Easter celebrations.

"So in the end, who got the building?" I asked. "The church or the atheists?"

"Oh, they're both still there, together," Slova answered. "The museum is in the basement and the church is on the upper floors." He paused and looked out the window. "Of course," he said, "only in Russia can the Central Cathedral and the Museum of Atheism share the same building."

He was right. It would be like having a Robert Mapplethorpe exhibition in the basement of St. Patrick's Cathedral in New York. Only in Russia.

Mirsky arrived at the Atrium. He had called to say he would take time to come and meet us. He told me how pleased he was with Slova. "*Toylko doveriye*," he said. "Only trust. I have complete faith in this man, and we are very happy with the work he has been doing."

It was a nice moment. I gave Mirsky the bottle of Archive Scotch I had bought, told him it had been an honor to work for him, and said I hoped he would enjoy it. As Mirsky got up to leave, Slova reached for the bottle.

"Not on your life," Mirsky said, snatching it away. "I am going to sign this bottle and it cannot be drunk until I say so."

Slova dropped his arm and bowed his head. He knew that "total trust" extended only so far.

It was nice that Mirsky had made that trip to see me in person. As he was walking out the door of the office, one of his staff said something to him that I didn't hear. Mirsky turned to him, and I did hear his answer.

"*Vsyo-taki, kakoe-to most on boyl.*" Just the same, he was a kind of bridge.

That could be my epitaph.

GLENN WILLIAMSON

learned Russian at Exeter, Georgetown, and Leningrad before earning a Chicago MBA. After the Berlin Wall and Chicago office markets both fell, he took on new developments in Eastern Europe. Williamson lives in Washington, DC, with his two sons and teaches real estate at Georgetown University.